City and Islington Sixth Form College
The Angel 283-309 Goswell Road
London EC1V 7LA
020 7520 0652

CITY AND ISLINGTON
COLLEGE

CHECK DVD AT BACK OF

This book is due for return on or before the date last stamped below.
You may renew by telephone. Please quote the Barcode No.
May not be renewed if required by another reader.

BOOK!

Fine: 5p per day

1 8 JAN 2008
1 2 OCT 2010

CPD6017

Learning Centre
City and Islington Sixth Form College
283-309 Goswell Road
London EC1V 7LA

Other Books by Geof Hewitt:

Poetry

I Think They'll Lay My Egg Tomorrow

Just Worlds

Living in Whales: Vermont Public School Stories & Poems (ed.)

Only What's Imagined

Poem & Other Poems

Quickly Aging Here: Some Poets of the 1970's (ed.)

Selected Poems of Alfred Starr Hamilton (ed.)

Stone Soup

Today You Are My Favorite Poet: Writing Poems with Teenagers

Writing Without Walls: Boise Writing in the Schools (ed. With James Hepworth)

Poems in Performance

The Maple Corner Tape: Poems from Vermont (with Chuck Meese)

Nonfiction

A Portfolio Primer: Teaching, Collecting, and Assessing Student Writing

Reading to Learn: A Classroom Guide to Reading Strategy Instruction (ed.)

Today You Are My Favorite Poet: Writing Poems with Teenagers

Working for Yourself

Geof Hewitt is available for in-service presentations and writing workshops through the Discover Writing Speakers Bureau. Contact: http://www.discover-writing.com/speakers.html

Discover Writing Press   www.discoverwriting.com   © 2005

HEWITT'S GUIDE
to SLAMPoetry
& PoetrySLAM

by Geof Hewitt

DVD ACTION GUIDE INCLUDED

DISCOVER WRITING PRESS

DISCOVER WRITING PRESS

PO Box 264
Shoreham, Vermont 05770
1-800-613-8055
www.discoverwriting.com

A Maureen O'Connor Burgess Design
Illustrations by Tim Newcomb

ISBN # 1-931492-09-3
Library of Congress Control Number: 2004195753

11 10 09 08 07 06 05   10 9 8 7 6 5 4 3 2

For more lesson plans and information on seminars, please visit our website at
www.discoverwriting.com <http://www.discoverwriting.com/>

For their help in the many phases of producing this book and the accompanying DVD, I want to thank Barry Lane, Sarah Bursky, Luis Dechtiar, Seth Jarvis, designer Maureen O'Connor Burgess, illustrator Tim Newcomb, the People's Republic of Vermont Poetry Slam Team, ElizabethThomas, Janet Lind Hewitt, and especially Leslie Taggart, editor extraordinaire.

Thanks, also, to all the poets, young and old alike, who offered their assistance by slamming in front of the camera as we filmed the DVD.

And to Vermont's teachers who have let me into their classrooms to experiment with all this madness: you are the best!

Discover Writing Press   www.discoverwriting.com   © 2005

our years ago, slam poetry came to Vermont and I was ready. For ten years I'd been hearing about slam, and on my occasional trips out of state I'd search the alternative newspapers for slams within a bus ride of my motel: I was always a day late or leaving town too soon.

So when Shannon Williams, a brilliant slammaster from Austin, Texas, came to Vermont and promoted the state's first-known official slam, to be held at Burlington's Rhombus Gallery on May 5, 1999, I was at the door, waiting to sign up, an hour before Shannon arrived to open the house.

It was a historic moment for me, even if your average person on the street can't name the date or even tell you what slam is. You see, I happened to win that slam, but no matter what the judges' decision, I'd have been hooked. This was the most fun – once it was written – I'd ever had with my poetry!

A year later, Vermont's first-ever statewide slam-offs found me in Burlington's City Hall, before an audience of three hundred, competing with fifteen other slammers who had also qualified in local events to compete for one of four places on the state team. During her short time in the state, Shannon Williams had firmly planted slam in Vermont.

I survived the first two of three elimination bouts, and selected my immortal poem, "The Ultimate Commute," for the final round: six slammers competing for the four spots on the team. It was a hot night and the slam had gone on for nearly three hours, but the house was still packed. Three hundred people hushed as scores were announced, then tallied, at the end of each performance. My 26.7 brought cheers: it was just high enough to ensure me the fourth position on the team.

My throat and chest clogged up with gloating, which I struggled to contain, until the time-keeper stepped forward with his heavy news. The poem ran three minutes and thirteen seconds, resulting in a half-point overtime penalty, sinking me from fourth place on Vermont's team to the honorary post of alternate.

I traveled to Providence for the Nationals and watched my teammates struggle through the bouts without me. At first I wished one of them, anyone, would get sick, so I could have a

PAGE
9

shot at one of the official venues. But I quickly discovered the sideshows throughout Providence: slams were everywhere! And everyone was invited to slam.

A year later I had reluctantly chewed off a few unnecessary lines and figured out a way to move my mouth, stuffed with the slightly shorter versions, a little faster, spitting out my poems within the three-minute time limit and winning a hotly contested place on Vermont's 2001 team. We flew to Seattle, slept five nights in a run-down motel (three of us in each of two rooms), and finished in the middle of the pack of nearly sixty teams from across the country. Competing in the Nationals is thrilling, and with so many poets all staying at the cheapest place in town, the party never ends.

In Seattle, before our bouts, several people asked me, in reference to my teammates, "Are you their coach?" Finally it struck me: Hello! At fifty-eight, I am significantly older than most slammers. It finally hit home why my teammates called me "Uncle Geof." Yet I like it that slam gives me a chance to relate to younger people not as a teacher, but as another poet trying hard to get the world to hear.

Discover Writing Press   www.discoverwriting.com   © 2005

In bars and church basements, in schools and in prisons, in parks, bookstores, and on street corners, slam is happening. What it all boils down to is poetry spoken by its author in three minutes or less, with audience members encouraged to cheer or boo and move freely throughout the event. Five members of that audience act as judges and please or annoy the audience with the power of their scoring. The scores are offered only as gut responses to the poet's performance and the poem. The judges don't know much about poetry: slam is for the people!

The term "slam" is just marketing hype, intended to convey attitude, illuminating its difference from a polite, gently applauded poetry reading. And it isn't all just poetry. Anything goes, as long as only the performer's voice and body are used — no props, no musical accompaniment. It's the judges' job to determine whether what's been presented qualifies as poetry.

In my first experiences with slam, I never considered its possible value in schools. In fact, I hesitated at the thought of promoting competition among youngsters, especially in relation to the gentle art of creating poetry: protect us from the competitive ethic that dominates sports; save us from competition brought openly to the classroom! This was certainly a suitable outlet for anyone, regardless of age (as I was inadvertently proving), but I dismissed my latest obsession as inappropriate for the classroom, at least until the high school years. This sparsely examined feeling prevailed even as I railed at teachers through my full-time job with the Vermont Department of Education to "Share your hobbies and obsessions with your students, who will help you find the necessary links to the 'standards' you are hired to help them meet and exceed."

Remember your favorite moments as a "pupil"? I'll bet they involved actually **doing something** or, perhaps during the inevitable teacher-centered "lessons" (lectures), they occurred when the teacher revealed something about his or her private life and special interests. The nearly mythic Miss Clough only taught us; that was her job. Her joyless task was twofold: to impart knowledge and maintain order.

But David Ray strayed from the job description, intent on being himself. He complained when he received only one Valentine card; he groused at the government; he shared his concerns about air quality. He read his poem of outrage (this was long before "the environment" became a popular issue) at people who leave their motors running at truck stops. When he felt the air

PAGE
11

was polluted he wore a facemask. He made no effort to quell rumors that had him running across a busy highway to be upwind of a speeding truck that nearly ran him down.

The "pupils" in Miss Clough's class were forever cutting up: Richard Lever would tear off chunks of his art gum eraser and propel them with his pencil across the room, where his best shots struck the billowing asbestos curtain above the radiator, emitting a sharp thwack that often occasioned Clough's famous remonstration: "I'll know who is doing that if I never, but I will," a nonsensical response that delighted us, repeated every time she was flustered in locating a culprit.

David's class encouraged playfulness, but with focus. Students, then or now, are lucky to have such teachers. Teachers who bring their songs to the classroom. Or who are fly fishers and, even though the class isn't biology, can discuss the strategies involved in encouraging trout to rise to the fly.

This belief in a teacher's sharing his or her deepest interests was a cornerstone of my pedagogical ethic. It's ironic that I was so reluctant to suggest a slam in the classroom, even though I happily described the phenomenon, encouraging students to make an effort to find a slam on their own.

And so I shocked myself a little at the final celebration of a day's poetry residency, when I heard myself offering a group of fourth and fifth graders a choice: "Hands up for those of you who'd like a traditional format for your poetry reading," versus "Let me see hands for those voting in favor of a slam." Of the eighty or so students sitting on the carpet of the little school's library, only four or five voted in favor of a reading, even though I had explained that fewer students could participate if they voted for a slam.

"We have only an hour before the buses leave, so we'll need to draw names from a hat if we slam," I explained. "Everyone can have a chance if you vote for a reading, but a slam uses up time while the judges are scoring and the scorekeeper is adding up the scores."

It didn't matter. They wanted to slam! Hands fluttered up from the library carpet like a massive flock of gulls startled off a tiny island. Adding to my surprise, more than half the students threw their names into the hat.

In the two years since, I've led slams and given slam workshops in classrooms with students as young as second grade. Only once have I wondered, after perhaps three dozen such work-

PAGE
12

shops, whether the competition tainted the experience of reading an original poem aloud, a regular component of my workshops until this conversion. In all but one classroom slam, the judging has been generous, the students wholly supportive of each other, the nonwinners cheerful and seemingly unbruised. I dare you to claim the same for football or soccer! In the exception, I called the sixth-grade teacher a couple of days later. "It seemed as if the student judges ganged up on that tall boy, each giving a rock-bottom score for a pretty good poem."

I heard him sigh over the phone. "It wouldn't have mattered whether we'd slammed or just shared our poems. They're always on his case: he's the brightest student in the class."

Any competitive activity can cause hurt feelings, which is why the slammaster repeatedly reminds audience, judges, and poets that the scoring is arbitrary, and it's the audience's job to try to influence the judges by cheering for the poems and booing scores that seem stingy.

During a daylong slam workshop with Bobbe Pennington's fifth-grade students, I saw the great care she showed for each child. I was not surprised when, in preparation for the afternoon slam that would climax the day, she took me aside to ask that I not encourage the audience to boo scores that seemed too harsh. "We want to teach good manners," she explained.

It was the third or fourth student who read his poem flawlessly, and apparently it's a poem Bobbe really likes, because when one of the judges gave it a three-point-seven, Bobbe broke the booing taboo and led a growing round of enthusiastic hissing and boos. "I guess I just forgot," she acknowledged later, but throughout the remainder of the slam, goodhearted sounds of exaggerated disapproval greeted low scores, balancing the cheers for scores well received.

A good slammaster can keep the atmosphere bright in the face of audience disdain, simply reminding everyone that the points don't really matter; it's the courage of the poets and the courage of the judges to stick to their beliefs that count.

Discover Writing Press   www.discoverwriting.com   © 2005

SLAM IN THE CLASSROOM
Chapter 1: Why Slam?

Often described as a cross between mud wrestling and a literary tea, slam invites participation on all levels. Not only does it help satisfy the requirements of a language arts curriculum, it offers a variety of related tasks, from stage manager to slammaster, marketing director to scorekeeper, that suggest the potential involvement of a broad group of young people.

At two Vermont high schools, I've seen slam thrive as a student-driven, extracurricular activity, not just something that happens in some of the language arts classes from which it originally sprang. The teachers have helped pave the way, then let the students take over. In Bristol, Mount Abraham students ran a monthly open slam at Rockydale Pizza for two or three years. For a while, at least, the management provided free pizza to anyone who slammed. In Montpelier, students at U-32 High School created a slam scene that overflowed the standing-room-only student commons. I still test the waters when I'm invited to guest teach in schools, tentatively introducing the possibility of celebrating our work with a real-life poetry slam. We don't want anyone's feelings hurt, so I carefully explain that luck, more than skill, often determines the winner.

"Luck?" the teacher asks.

"Yes," I reply, "a lot depends on your place in the order of performance, the mood created by the poem that's presented just before yours, and the fact that the judges are amateurs, chosen at random from the audience. They represent the people! With little sophistication in matters poetic, their judgments are unpredictable, and should never be taken too seriously. Not only that, but the scores almost always get higher as the slam progresses. The first few slammers rarely make it to the finals."

Understanding the role of luck and the somewhat arbitrary nature of the judging mitigates the sting of defeat. A good slammaster frequently reminds the crowd that the competition is not

what matters. Indeed, it is the slammaster's job to select judges who claim no expertise in poetry, and to highlight this fact from the stage when introducing them to the audience. Having screened a candidate for conflict of interest, the slammaster asks, "What qualifies you to be a judge?" The responses, quoted verbatim from the stage, can set just the right tone for the "competition" to follow: "Our next judge is Sally, who says she's qualified because she's never been to a slam and usually doesn't read poetry. Let's have a hand for Sally!"

Indeed, slam organizers often emphasize the hype of slam as integral to the event: the scoring is but a gimmick to draw a crowd. The three-minute performance limit generally ensures that no given poet will go on for longer than one might hold one's breath in four or five consecutive gasps. Not only a kindness to the audience, the time limit also benefits the performers: knowing that each poet will be onstage for a limited period, the audience pays careful attention — at least to the poet's first few lines.

Exhorting the audience to respond to the poems with cheers and, as desired, to cheer or boo the judges' scores, ensures opportunity for everyone to become involved, and eliminates the uncomfortable formality of a traditional poetry reading. The slammaster who whips up the audience honors the spirit of slam, which is to emphasize the nature of poetry as a democratic art, of and for the people, not the province of some self-proclaimed literary elite. As Burlington slammaster Kim Jordan says, "You'll often hear snoring at a poetry reading, but no one sleeps at a slam!"

A noisy crowd serves a double benefit: spontaneous cheering and periodic booing attract the attention of passersby and swell the audience. In fact, the audience is as important as the poets who read or perform their work. Slam creates community and depends on it, usually attracting its regulars among local poets who, like me, may be a little frustrated by the anonymity, the invisibility, of the readers of any work that may have found its way into print. Through slam, a writer gets immediate and obvious response to the ideas and fantasies that a poem may convey.

I suppose the same might be said for poetry readings. Don't they, too, give the author immediate, face-to-face response? Yes, but. Poetry readings are usually somewhat restrained affairs where the audience sits on its hands and everyone breathes quietly (except for those who may be snoring). The format of traditional poetry readings is the culprit: without a three-minute time limit, a poet's voice often turns to background noise, even when the poems, on the page, produce goosebumps. Of course there are exceptions, readings featuring just one poet who goes on for hours and receives cheers after nearly every poem.

And I'll admit that there are slams where you'd rather be somewhere else, doing something else – maybe at home, chewing on aluminum foil. This book intends to eliminate that possibility.

In summary, the slammaster's job is to keep the event moving right along, exhorting the audience to cheer the poets and their poems, to boo when the judging seems stingy, and to remember that an audience's contribution to the event makes the real difference between a literary slumberfest and a good time for all.

Good News for the School Board

Given that it invites such broad participation, let's look at slam from the perspective of an education administrator or school board member, concerned about standards. Slam of course encourages creative composition, so it meets many of the curriculum's "Communication" or "Writing" standards, but it also calls on speaking and listening skills, the bane of all who would seek a way to assess the whole of language arts and communication. Slam requires skills for which we have no rubrics, at least not yet, but that we do, indeed, seek to teach. Speaking and listening make up half the traditional language arts curriculum. Reading and writing are the other half, and slam involves all four: slam instruction could arguably occupy most if not all of an English/language arts classroom's time.

Slam offers a refreshing break to the teacher, and to the student whose usual writing assignments are returned with corrections. Slam thus offers the teacher a vacation from collecting and responding to the written work in favor of listening. Knowing that the teacher isn't going to see the written product, some students actually write better than when trepidation squeezes away all hope of fluency. When a student, uninterested in the standard curriculum, finds slam as a way to express disaffection, a fresh bond forms between that student and academic pursuits.

Perhaps the thrill of slam is the unexpected, as well as the knowledge that slam is about unbridled expression. A school's guidelines may prohibit certain language or content, but the encouragement of attitude, the informal to rowdy nature of the good-hearted competition, and (if allowed) unbridled expression, often draw the attention of students who are otherwise

uninterested in reading or writing, public speaking or theater.

Theater! You bet. Not just in the sense of performance, but in all that goes with theater production. A student who cares only about electronics can be harnessed to provide lighting and sound, the mathematician can tally the scores, the administrator can promote the slam, the class clown can be slammaster: each will play a role that draws them into a theater community. Each will also see and hear classmates who engage in heartfelt, if sometimes artless expression. There's nothing like being witness to another's courage in "standing up for one's poem," in triumphant and maybe especially in disastrous performances. Whatever role a student is playing, whether as audience member or technician, there's always a chance that this exposure to others' virtuosity will inspire, or that the witnessing of courage, triumph, or disaster will occasion the thought: "I could do better than that!" Or, at least, "I could do that!"

Hooking the Outriders

Because attitude in all its forms is honored at slams, even the most disenfranchised students sometimes find an avenue for active participation. This can open the door to friendships among geeks, jocks, and grade grubbers, and for those students who have drifted into alienation, it can show the way to wider participation in healthy activities.

Another feature that contributes to slam's broad attraction is the variety of styles of poetry that take home the big prizes. Attend more than one neighborhood- or school-based slam, and you'll see that, on any given occasion, a sonnet may conquer a hip-hop rant, or that a stream-of-consciousness, barely coherent spitfire of words can top the most carefully articulated sestina. Where slams are offered on a regular basis, some poets develop unique performance personas, often writing poems in the voice of the chosen persona. After four or five slams, a poet may realize the old persona needs updating, and a fresh style of poem begins to emerge. Especially with young writers, I want to remember to teach persona and to address all my responses to "the narrator" of the poem. This enhances the writer's understanding that imagination has no limits and that what the poem presents does not necessarily reflect on the poet. Sometimes this opens the door for confessional writing, which I address in Chapter 5.

Atmosphere and Ownership

In creating an "anything goes that doesn't embarrass or hurt feelings" atmosphere, the slam-master reminds performers that hamming it up is okay, that showing an attitude may result in a higher score than presenting the poem in an objective voice. Experimenting with one's "style" is encouraged. A good poem may naturally evoke some enthusiasm or dramatic movement from its author. This is encouraged in slam, and it follows that performing a poem off book frees the hands for gesture, and allows the eyes to make specific, focused contact with members of the audience. (See Chapter 6 for exercises to help students develop meaningful eye contact.) Let's face it: a slammer is trying to sell the poem. Any salesperson will tell you that good eye contact works its magic two ways. It helps the buyer to believe the seller is honest, and it tells the seller whether the buyer is hearing the pitch. For this reason, I prefer venues that let the slammers see the audience and, if I have any sway with the stage manager, I ask for enough house lighting so the poets can see whether anyone at all is listening. Under these conditions, a good performer can virtually compel the audience to pay attention. And what the slammer sees on the faces out there can surely influence the performance, sometimes even the choice of words.

In venues where the performer must slam into darkness, receiving audience feedback is a little more challenging: one must attend to the sounds emanating from the audience. (If there's a lot of coughing, you're in trouble!) Without house lights, the joy of seeing what's happening is obliterated, so even though a darkened theater may provide the optimum dramatic impact, for the slammers' sake ask for a modest amount of house lighting.

In spite of my own preferences when it's time for me to slam, I would always want slam to be student owned – which brings up a paradox in a book like this for teachers: How can we nurture slam in our schools, perhaps playing a lead role in getting it started, then back away so the students take control and come to own the program?

Each reader can plot his or her way to success in this effort. My own strategy would be and is to participate in any slam I can get into, and excuse myself from organizational responsibilities, saying, "Why, that would be a conflict of interest, since I intend to compete!" That works for me, and of course I encourage any teacher who would support students' writing and/or performing to be out there writing and performing too. Do that one thing, take the same risks you ask of your students – and there's no wrong you can do, even as a teacher. If we do not model the efforts we exhort from our students, how can we be seen as anything but taskmasters!

Discover Writing Press   www.discoverwriting.com   © 2005

Chapter 2: A Short History of Slam

In the early 1980s Marc Smith, a Chicago construction worker, struggled, as many poets do, with the fact that his friends showed little interest in his poetry. He persuaded the manager of a local jazz club to let him host an open mike night, where performance poets would find a ready opportunity to voice their work. A couple of years later, Smith approached the owner of The Green Mill, another popular Chicago watering hole, with the idea of a weekly performance poetry competition, calling it a "Poetry Slam." On July 25, 1986, the Uptown Poetry Slam was born, the first of an on-going series of Sunday night bouts for The Green Mill and a milestone in the history of U.S. poetry.

The element of competition, the venue, the fact that Smith wanted audience members to feel free to move about whenever they wished, plus the fact that audience members were instructed to respond to the competitors and to the judges in any way they saw fit – these components created an irreverent setting where, it seems, outrageousness often triumphed over quality. Yet its proponents claimed that slam was the most democratic form of poetry: anyone is eligible to compete, and any person is eligible to serve as a judge.

Before long, slam spread from Chicago to Ann Arbor; New York; San Francisco; Fairbanks, Alaska; Boston; Austin; Providence; Seattle; San Antonio; Pittsburgh; Ithaca, New York, and beyond until, in 1999, it arrived in Burlington, Vermont.

Each summer, the National Poetry Slam hosts teams of five or six poets (four competitors, an alternate, and often a coach) for a long weekend of intensive slamming. Members of each team must have won their positions through a certified, annual spring slam-off in their home region. In recent years, fifty teams or more have competed for the national title, and organizers have been scrambling to determine a fair way to keep the number of teams from becoming unmanageable. New guidelines now establish a separate national slam for solo slammers, the "Independents."

Just like the National Slam, which normally welcomes poets of all ages, a national youth slam, "Brave New Voices," is held each spring somewhere in the United States. As popular as the Nationals, Brave New Voices attracts teams from across the country and sometimes from abroad. Teachers who escort young people to Brave New Voices often mention the unusual opportunity students have to meet fellow-poets "from all over." They also praise the organizers of the event for minimizing the competitive aspects of slam, even to the point of presenting "congeniality" awards to teams that show exceptional sportspersonship!

For information on Brave New Voices, go to www.upwordspoetry.com. To locate slams near you, try www.poetryslam.com for a list of more than one hundred slam venues across the country. Check alternative newspapers, library and bookstore bulletin boards, attend a well-publicized poetry reading and ask around. Or, go ahead, start a slam yourself!

Chapter 3: Organizing and Hosting a Slam

To prepare for a slam, organizers need to consider the following, essential details:

- The venue, which can vary from a church basement to a restaurant to a high school gymnasium or classroom.
- Publicity, such as posters, press releases, phone calls, and word of mouth.
- A slammaster or host responsible for appointing judges and emceeing the event, keeping the audience revved up and the show moving.
- Someone who will watch the door if there's an admission fee (often the source of the cash prizes).
- Rules and procedures for the slam, including sign-up protocols that keep the number of slammers reasonable – twelve or fifteen poets, tops!

While some slams offer special themes or feature specific exceptions to the rules, a typical slam adheres to the three-minute time limit, and prohibits costumes, props, and musical accompaniment. Anything else, as long as the poet is performing original work, is fine. Most often there's a modest fee at the door: everyone, including the slammers, pays a few bucks to support the event and to subsidize modest prizes.

Slammers arrive early to sign up. When too many competitors have registered, their names usually go into a hat, which is also a good way to determine the sequence of performances. The higher one's number, the better that person's luck, since scores tend to become more generous – a phenomenon known as "score creep" – as the event progresses.

The Slammaster

The slammaster, host of the event, is responsible for all details, the most important of which is delegating responsibility. While gathering the names of all eligible slammers, the slammaster recruits and interviews potential judges. Sometimes an audience member who is reluctant to judge will acquiesce when offered the chance to work with a partner. Many slams wind up with a mixture of single and paired judges. The slammaster must also recruit a timekeeper, a scorekeeper, and a "sacrificial poet."

Selecting Judges

Selecting judges, the slammaster first ensures that no one has a conflict of interest, that a judge won't disappear before a round has been completed, and that each judge provides a snippet of personal information regarding his or her relationship to slams or to poetry: "Do you favor any of tonight's slammers?" is a good question with which to approach a potential judge. Only if the answer is "no" should one ask whether that person would like to serve as a judge.

"Do you promise to remain a judge at least through the first complete round?" If a second round is part of the plan, the slam-master can always appoint a new judge or group of judges. This provides fresh perspectives and limits the effects of any hidden favoritism.

"What is your name, and what qualifies you to be a judge?" At this point, the slammaster should take notes, jotting down anything that emphasizes the judge's lack of expertise. When a judge has no response to the qualification question, feel free to suggest words that suggest incompetence, a face-saving detail for the poets who are not among the top scorers. "Oh, you're qualified because you've never judged before!" usually works.

The next factor in selecting judges is their placement in the room. One wants judges from the back and front, the left and right, and the center of the audience. In establishing judgeship, hand out thick markers and a good supply of paper, encouraging the judges to "Write big!" or give each judge two identical stacks of ten cards each, numbered 0 to 9 (one stack for the whole number, one for the decimal place) with careful instructions not to "reverse" the scores, lest an enthusiastic score of 9.1 be displayed as a 1.9. Should a judge inadvertently display reversed cards, the slammaster can joke about the judge's disregard for protocol. "Once a rebel, always a rebel!"

Of course, that troublesome decimal point might be eliminated if people realized it would be easier

to report scores on a scale of 0 to 100, but this wouldn't be as much fun, since the decimal point suggests finite precision. Appointing judges, I emphasize the significance of the decimal point, especially when judges are paired, one offering the whole point score and the second holding up the decimal score. Anyone who questions the importance of the decimal hasn't considered life's true realities – as in an Olympic event, where .0001 second can mean the difference between a gold medal and a silver or bronze, that seemingly arbitrary decimal score can have terrific significance!

Rehearsing the Judges

Once judges have been appointed, the slammaster should take the stage to ensure that the scorecards are visible, asking each judge to "Show the cards" or "Hold 'em!" One might even ask the judges to rehearse a simultaneous display of scores. "Okay, judges, pretend that each of you wants to score the performance as an 8.9. Get those scores ready. Fast. Now: One, two, three, hold 'em!"

Run through this exercise four or five times, altering the requested scores each time, and you'll have a group of trained judges, ready to accommodate the requirements of fumble-free, simultaneous scoring! This will keep the slam moving and can even provide fodder for the slammaster's patter. "Great simultaneous scoring! Let's hear it for these talented judges!"

But if you have a slow judge, or if you cannot, from the stage, perceive the difference between a six and an eight, the slam will drag. So don't overlook these details. Your slam's success depends on them.

Formal instructions to the judges can wait for the beginning of the slam, when the slammaster explains the rules of the game (see inside front cover) to all competitors, audience, judges, timekeeper, and scorekeeper alike.

The Timekeeper

The timekeeper watches the clock on every performance, but like a tennis umpire, only speaks when a "fault" has been committed and, lest knowledge of a time infraction influence decisions, only after the scorekeeper has tallied the judges' scores. This provides special drama, a rare opportunity for the timekeeper to show some power over the proceedings. As mentioned earlier, a slammer may perform without penalty for three minutes and a ten-second grace period. There is no warning bell! For every ten-second block or portion thereof beyond three minutes and ten seconds, the scorekeeper must deduct a half point from the slammer's total score. The timekeeper, who can expect to receive jeers from the audience, announces the total number of seconds beyond the grace period that the performance went overtime: **"Oh, Slammaster, the poem exceeded the grace period by twenty-one seconds."** Even without a calculator, the slammaster can then regretfully instruct the scorekeeper to deduct one-and-a-half points from the final score, each ten seconds or portion thereof resulting in a half-point penalty.

The clock starts with the slammer's first utterance or significant gesture, and stops with the final utterance. Thus, it is unwise, unless he or she has a short poem, for a slammer to speak to the audience before presenting the poem. Introductory remarks are almost always redundant anyway! As for "significant gestures," the timekeeper must use discretion. Certainly, adjusting a microphone or laying one's manuscript on the floor is no "significant gesture," but pre-performance miming, such as winking at a judge or wiping imaginary flopsweat from one's brow, usually triggers the stopwatch.

The Scorekeeper

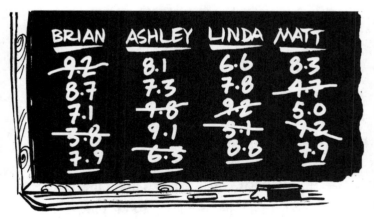

The scorekeeper sits at a table in the front of the room, with a chalkboard or easel and newsprint, visible to the audience, upon which the names of the slammers have been written in the order that the slammaster plucked their names from the hat. Some scorekeepers use a calculator, and at many slams, because accuracy often plays second fiddle to speed, a second scorekeeper tallies the judges' scores independently and compares results before the scorekeeper calls out a total score. The scorekeeper then writes that score on the chalkboard or newsprint for all to see as the slammaster repeats it from the stage.

The Sacrificial Poet

The sacrificial poet, also referred to as the "calibration poet," opens the show, offering a poem not only to warm up the audience but also for the judges' benefit. The scores they assign to the sacrificial poet have no consequence in the sense of competition, but serve as benchmark scores; the judges score each ensuing performance relative to the score they gave the sacrificial poet. As a kindness, it's a good idea to explain score creep to the sacrificial poet, who may otherwise suffer hurt feelings if his/her score is repeatedly topped throughout the slam.

The Slam Begins

The slam begins with the slammaster introducing him/herself, sometimes presenting a poem (which is not scored) or otherwise engaging in light banter as the audience settles. Then, with great ceremony, the slammaster introduces the timekeeper, the scorekeeper, and each of the judges, encouraging enthusiastic applause for each of these important officials, but to stress the folly of scoring poetry, taking care to offer a quote from each judge that emphasizes at least a measure of incompetence.

> "These judges, carefully screened to ensure that they have no conflict of interest, will each present scores, zero to ten with one decimal point, a zero signifying the worst piece of drivel imaginable, and a ten indicating a poem and performance that tore a judge's socks off and blew them to Tahiti. I have tirelessly interviewed the judges to determine their overall ignorance of poetry; they will base their scores half on the content of the poem, half on the quality of the performance. Now, judges, this needs to be a gut reaction, not something that requires five minutes of deliberation. I'll want your scores fast, so get your scorecards ready and remember always to judge each slammer relative to the score you gave to the sacrificial poet! "

Discover Writing Press   www.discoverwriting.com   © 2005

Many slammasters ask for a show of hands from audience members who are attending their first slam. **"Aha! We have many newcomers with us. Let's have a round of applause for these neophytes. For their benefit, I shall present the rules of tonight's event."**

Here it is especially important to announce the overall structure of the slam:

> **Will it be one, two, or three rounds?**
>
> **How will a slammer qualify to perform in rounds two and three?**
>
> **How was the order of performance determined for round one, and how will it be decided for rounds two and three?**
>
> **Will the winners be determined by totaling their scores from all rounds, or only by their score in the final round?**

Overlooking these details can result in confusion and, sometimes, hard feelings, so it's a good idea to review them with the competitors before the slam, then repeat them from the stage for the benefit of all:

> **"Tonight we have twelve slammers and a sacrificial poet. This is a three-round elimination bout with cumulative scoring. In round one, our twelve slammers will compete in the order their names came out of the hat. The top-scoring six slammers from round one will enter round two in reverse order from their positions in round one. Four poets will survive round two to compete in the final round, for which I will again determine sequence by drawing names. As I said, scoring is cumulative throughout the event: the winners of rounds two and three will be determined by their cumulative scores."**

Instructions for the Audience

Next comes a charge to the audience, which can go something like this:

"The judges will be rock solid, unswerving in their decisions. Their job is never to abandon their duty as objective observers, never to let the audience influence their scoring. And it is the audience's job to influence the judges. If you like a poem, let the judges know it! If you don't like a judge's score, let the judge know how you feel! Judges, you must ignore the audience's response! By the way, folks, don't forget to cheer the poets!"

The Sacrificial Poet Takes the Stage

"And now, without further comment, here is our sacrificial poet, coming all the way from Essex Junction, the one and only Patricia Ann SMEDLEY!"

Like any good huckster, the slammaster pitches the voice in such a way as to guarantee copious applause, perhaps even catcalls, whistling, and cheers, as the sacrificial poet takes the stage.

As soon as a performance ends, the slammaster is onstage, exhorting the judges to

"Hurry up, get with it, you only have another five seconds before I call for your scores. … Okay, one, two, three: Judges, show your scores!"

Discover Writing Press   www.discoverwriting.com   © 2005

Ideally, the scorecards go up simultaneously, and the slammaster encourages the audience to cheer or boo as he/she reports the numbers.

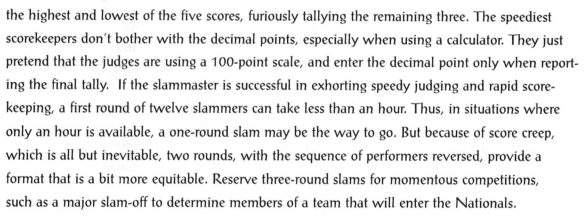

> "Three point two! What do you think of that, audience?"
> "And a nine point seven, wow!"

The scorekeeper records the numbers, rushing to discard the highest and lowest of the five scores, furiously tallying the remaining three. The speediest scorekeepers don't bother with the decimal points, especially when using a calculator. They just pretend that the judges are using a 100-point scale, and enter the decimal point only when reporting the final tally. If the slammaster is successful in exhorting speedy judging and rapid scorekeeping, a first round of twelve slammers can take less than an hour. Thus, in situations where only an hour is available, a one-round slam may be the way to go. But because of score creep, which is all but inevitable, two rounds, with the sequence of performers reversed, provide a format that is a bit more equitable. Reserve three-round slams for momentous competitions, such as a major slam-off to determine members of a team that will enter the Nationals.

As seriously as I emphasize the notion of working with a firm and mutual understanding of a slam's ground rules, I want to reiterate that the slammaster's job is to keep the event lighthearted, and to highlight the somewhat arbitrary nature of the competition.

Clarifying the Rules: A Cautionary Tale

Sometimes the simplest details fall by the wayside, causing unnecessary heartache and distress. It is far easier to keep the competition lighthearted when everyone understands the rules. "How will we determine the winners!" needs advance consideration lest energy-draining discussions and half-baked decisions rob a slam of its good feeling.

The options multiply in slams that involve two or three rounds. If this is an elimination slam, how many poets will continue from one round to another? What will happen if there are ties? Additionally, everyone should understand the method of determining the sequence of performances in each round. Will the winner be determined by a cumulative total of his or her scores from all rounds, or will the winner be the slammer who survives one or two elimination rounds, then wins the final round?

Slammers may well adjust their strategies to take advantage of a particular slam's structure. One might perform his or her best piece in the first round of an elimination bout where scoring is cumulative, but save that poem for the final round if the final round alone determines the winner.

In 2001, the rules for Vermont's slam-off to determine the members of the state team were not carefully thought out. Everyone knew it was a three-round elimination bout, and that six poets would survive to compete in the final round. The slammaster brought the winners of that round to the stage, the audience cheered Vermont's brand-new 2001 slam team, and the evening was over. The audience went home as members of the team congratulated one another and consoled those who hadn't quite reached the winners' circle. Meanwhile, the fifth-place team "alternate" sat down with paper and pencil and totaled the scores of each of the six poets who had reached the final round. All along, he'd believed that the evening's results would be based on cumulative scores, and his math showed that if cumulative scores were in effect, he should have won fourth place, the last of the coveted performance slots.

An emergency meeting of the six finalists determined that we should hold a "super slam-off" two weeks later, in which all six of us would compete anew for our places on the team. I didn't like it, because I was at risk of losing my spot. But other poets on the team had bigger hearts, and seemed happy, in the name of fairness, to gamble their positions on the team. As I recall, we agreed to cumulative scores in a two-round nonelimination bout. Much to my relief, the first three places went, in the same order, to the same poets who had won the first three places in the disputed slam, but the poets originally in the fourth and alternate spots wound up switching places from what had been announced from the stage two weeks earlier as the "final" results.

The poet who was displaced from fourth place to the alternate's position remained cheerful throughout, saying, "I'm just happy to have a chance to travel with the team!" **Now that is the spirit of slam!**

Discover Writing Press   www.discoverwriting.com   © 2005

Chapter 4: No Boundaries: Variations on Traditional Slam

Slam is more a matter of spirit than "the rules," so slam accommodates virtually any variations, as long as the audience feels comfortable and is participating in a meaningful way. Given the possibility of judges working in pairs, judging involves ten people at most, and a couple of other audience members can serve as time and score keepers, respectively; it's the poets' and the slammaster's job to involve the others.

Because of the nature of scoring, I don't advise tampering with the five-scores rule. Fewer than five results in only one or two scores to total, after the highest and lowest have been discarded, and the weighting of the scores is too heavy on each of the one or two remaining scores. And fewer audience members are given a chance for involvement as judges. Add judges to the magic five and you'll chew up time collecting and tabulating those extra scores, a drag on the show. Instead of offering extra judgeships, pair people up, asking one member of each pair to vote the whole number, the other to vote the decimal point.

Beyond the number of judges, I can think of no other component of the traditional slam format that is sacrosanct. I've participated in about a dozen variations that have worked well, but turn a bunch of eager students loose with the possibilities, and I'm sure they can devise at least a dozen more. And many of the variations I'm suggesting here can be combined or altered to suit their own special circumstances!

The time limit can be manipulated, usually by shortening it. A one-minute slam will double the number of performance opportunities for potential slammers.

Cover slams: Instead of original poems, slammers perform someone else's work. This could be combined with the one-minute slam idea, with students sent to libraries and bookstores in search of short, performable poems.

Team slams: Instead of solo performances, form teams of two, three, or four poets to write and perform group pieces.

Déjà vu slams: Poets making it to the second round must perform the same poem they presented in round one. The variations and resulting effects of the second-round performances can be startling.

Prop slams: Each slammer may use one prop during the performance. (Limiting the number of props helps provide focus.)

Music slams: Slammers may use musical accompaniment, their own or that of one other person.

Benefit slams: Winners donate their prizes to a cause of their choice.

Prose slams: Who's to say that most of what gets performed in slams isn't prose, anyway! But specifying "prose" may open the door to some reluctant story or essay writers.

Form slams: My favorite of these is the Haiku Slam, one of the great sideshows at the National Poetry Slam, held each year in a different U.S. city. As it is staged at the Nationals, two slammers at a time, each armed with seven original haiku, go head-to-head in an elimination bout, alternating in being first or second poet to read in each "round." First slammer to win four rounds proceeds to the next bout until all but one of sixteen haiku slammers are eliminated.

This is just one example of how the rules and procedures of slam can be altered to suit the form or theme of the slam. The suddenness of haiku argues for the head-to-head drama, whereas the longer forms (try a **Sonnet** or **Sestina Slam!**) are better suited to the normal sequencing of all eligible slammers competing in a round.

Newcomers', Veterans', Teachers', Chick or Macho Slams: Name your classification. The only danger is becoming so rarefied that not enough poets will consider themselves eligible.

Anything Goes Slams: The only limitation here is the three-minute rule. Otherwise, yes, "Anything Goes"! This invites props, music, prose, and all possible variations on these "Variations."

PAGE
34

Freestyling: Performers invent the poem on the spot, usually in response to a topic drawn from a hat, called out by the audience, or dictated by the slammaster.

Theme slams: Any academic discipline has its themes, so theme slams work well to encourage poetry writing across the curriculum. But overarching themes are also terrific fodder for writing and performing. Themes based on a novel or popular movie also work well.

During a visit to Chicago in 1999, still new to slamming, I asked my host, playwright/poet David Schein, if he knew of any nearby slams. Two hours later we were perched on stools at The Mad Bar, where I had just registered to participate in the evening's competition.

Names were drawn from a hat, and mine was the second of the ten or twelve slammers who had signed up. The slammaster took the stage and introduced the first slammer, adding the words, "Of course, as everyone already knows, tonight's theme is **Star Wars.**"

Everyone knows! Hardly. But if I were to admit ignorance, I might be eliminated from the slam, so as the evening's first slammer performed a hilarious rendition of R2D2's off-camera love affair, I racked my memory for the characters or features of a movie I'd seen fifteen years earlier and hadn't thought much about since. "Princess Leia!" "Obi-Wan Kenobi!"

Three minutes later I was onstage with the poem I'd planned to slam, with only one modification: the waitress in the poem would have a Princess Leia hairdo, and sometime later in the performance, I'd insert "Obi-Wan Kenobi," perhaps as an epithet, as in "Holy Obi Kenobi!" I accomplished these tasks in a flawless rendering of my famous poem "Passing Thru," and returned to my barstool next to David as the applause quickly sputtered out and the slammaster returned to the microphone.

"Thank you Geof, from Vermont. Do Not Go Gentle into That **Darth** Night!"

As the audience laughed at the slammaster's astute observation, David leaned from his barstool to speak directly into my ear: "I think he's got your number."

Chapter 5: Generating and Performing "Slam Poems"

The title of this chapter uses quotation marks to indicate that a "slam poem" is any piece of writing that uses only the human voice, facial expression and gesture, and takes no longer than three minutes to perform. Anything from a series of grunts to the tender reflection of a rhymed Petrarchan sonnet is, at least potentially, a "slam poem."

Certain types of poems, however, generally do not score high enough to place the slammer in a front-running position. Short poems, I have found, do not score well, probably because the audience (and the judges) need time to adjust to the slammer's voice and personality, and to the persona of the poem. Equally questionable are poems where visual puns are at the heart of the poem's meaning. So I doubt that a poem like my "Typographical Errors" would ever score above a three. Not only is it too short to give the judges a feel for the poem's persona, it relies on the correspondence of the title with the visual similarity of "words" and "worlds."

Typographical Errors
Don't let them bother you, she said.
After all, those are just worlds.

Okay, some poems slam better than others! Still, it's fun to compose work that challenges prevailing stereotypes of "slam" as well as poems that, for instance, capture the rhythms of hip-hop, or that express strongly held political views, or whatever else one can think of as a "slam poem." The more types of writing the better, as the poet adds to a stack of available manuscripts from which to pluck just the right poem at just the right time. My number two strategy (number one is trying to avoid time penalties) lies in the hope of capturing some turf that no other performer has trod upon, a poem from the heart in an event dominated by cynicism, or vice versa.

Essential Qualities for Slam Poems

Almost any poem-writing exercise can lead to a good slam poem, but it often helps the writer to keep in mind certain qualities of performance that are necessities or, at the least, enhancements to slam poems.

- The audience must be able to hear and understand the words. Especially during revision, a poet should consider the distinct sounds of words and phrases. Would it be easier to say "this fellow" than "this guy," which might be heard as "the sky"? Should "them all" be replaced with "everyone," lest the audience hear "the mall"?

- A good poem often suggests gesture and facial expression. While composing, be willing to "act the voice" of the poem, consciously changing facial expressions or gesturing as appropriate. David Schein claims that when he is drafting a play he is aware of his face changing to fit the character whose lines he is writing.

- The slammer can and probably should take on the character of the narrator of the poem, and good narrators usually present their tales with attitude. Thinking of various attitudes, from trusting to suspicious to sly to evasive to dishonest to silly to wondrous to angry to happy to sad to sarcastic to reverential to pleading to obsequious to bullying to apologetic, one realizes the powerful implications that can be communicated with thoughtful word choice joined to artful performance.

- A good poem often evokes more than one emotion. It's especially important to encourage students to recognize this possibility, because consciously switching emotions during composition or changing the narrator's attitude can create marvelous contrast or possible surprise. And sometimes this type of transition results in an entirely new poem!

Narrative Structure

I prefer narrative to lyric poems, which may be one reason I enjoy slams. Successful slam poems almost always have a narrative thread, something for the audience to grab on to. That thread can be established by a strong persona, someone with a story to tell. It might be how he or she was wronged or a self-aggrandizing account of the narrator's heroic actions or an evocation of a time the narrator witnessed a historic moment. What matters here are the dramatic details of the story, and their apparent impact on the person that the audience is seeing onstage.

If words, actions, gestures, and facial expressions create a strong sense of character, a slammer can also convey a narrative sense without story. List poems sometimes work well in this context, usually evoking laughter. "The things I want for my birthday" or "Thirty Memorable Embarrassing Moments" or, to suggest a more serious possibility: "Moments I wish I could forget." In composing such poems, the writer should remember the use of persona: autobiography is not necessarily required!

Another approach might be the breakfast-to-bed, chronological sequence of the narrator's typical day. Again, this could be a list poem, but it also might be generated by a strong rhythmic consideration:

> I stumble from bed every morning,
> And stare at my feet on the floor,
> I scramble the eggs and pour orange juice
> Drink my coffee and head out the door.

Persona

I cannot emphasize the power of persona enough. This should not be a guessing game, though sometimes it becomes one. Instead, persona requires the conscious acceptance of empathy, the willingness to explore the feelings and experiences of an imagined narrator, and, in slam, the ability to enact that persona for three minutes without making explicit reference to it. In place of announcing, "Here is my impression of an old man," the poem and poet need to be that old man.

Students who are not accustomed to persona might benefit from a brief investigation of the possibilities. Brainstorming personas in the classroom, ask students to call out a list of professions, then a set of circumstances, and finally a list of adjectives that suggest attitude. Write these in columns on the chalkboard, taking dictation as fast as the students can call out suggestions. In a center column, first list the professions. Next, to the right of that column, enter the circumstances. If a teacher follows this sequence, the students' ideas are fresher, more startling than if one brainstorms in a predictable sequence. The final list, adjectives to suggest attitude, is entered to the left of the center column. Thus, one has a frustrated dentist who has just won the lottery. Or, choose one from each column, not necessarily selecting the entries that are on the same horizontal plane!

The persona of a poem can be based on this list, but this is just a warm-up exercise, so ask each student to write a single phrase that their persona might say, have them speak it, then invite others to attempt to speak the same phrase in the same persona, then to try the same phrase in a different persona. The way a frustrated dentist who has just won a lottery would say "I'm on my way to Florida" would be different from a cranky, retired banker on her deathbed saying the same words. Like slam itself, conduct this exercise in a lighthearted and playful way.

Discover Writing Press   www.discoverwriting.com   © 2005

3 Attitude	1 Profession	2 Situation
frustrated	dentist	wins lottery
proud	teacher	visits Mexico
ditzy	cop	hitchhikes
clumsy	beggar	has heart attack

Confessional Poems

One danger teachers face is that a student, suddenly encouraged to write from the heart, may disclose information that suggests that he or she is in personal jeopardy. "Confessional" poems that are clearly autobiographical, as well as poems written in persona, can raise these issues. The best advice I've heard is to discuss with students, the first day of any class that involves "creative writing," the school's policy regarding the involvement of guidance counselors or social services. "If I learn something about you that makes me worry for your well-being, the law requires that I report it to the office."

The Fulcrum

Perhaps the simplest poetry concepts are all one needs. The idea of a fulcrum, a crucial point of balance or leverage, may be key in fashioning poems and stories that can hold an audience. The "balance" implied in my definition of "fulcrum" is not intended to break a poem into equal halves, but to leverage the power of the poem's final lines, in a sense "the moral of the story" or punch line, but subtly suggested by a narrowed focus on specific detail or a shift in attitude or both.

It might also be a change of perspective, a change of language, an explanation of something in contrast to the preceding topic, the resolution of a problem, a question in opposition to

preceding declaratives or vice versa, a shift of person or verb tense. Even a cliché might operate in contrast to the original language that has preceded it.

Things I Want for My Birthday

a 1955 Porsche Boxster with an airfoil
5 acres of land on the Maine coast a few miles from Bath
enough money to pay taxes on my land
someone to peel grapes for me full time
two perfect children who never forget my birthday
a canary that sings when I am lonely
a winding road to where we are this evening.

I admit to borrowing the last line of the above poem from Alfred Starr Hamilton's "April Lights." Sometimes using language from another source, not just a poem but perhaps a newspaper headline or a line from a popular song, can help the writer find the necessary shift.

Shortcuts to thinking this way may also be found by building on short exercises in contrast. Again, keeping the possibility of persona in mind, try:

> **Then, I ...**
> **Now, I ...**

or:

> **My question then was ...**
> **My question now is ...**

or:

> **If I could ...**
> **I would ...**

Typically, this type of short exercise leads to brief, fill-in-the-blank responses:

> **Then, I wore red dresses,**
> **Now, I wear old blue jeans.**

Encourage students to extend the images they have created, providing fresh detail that adds poignancy:

> **Then, I wore red dresses and lipstick to match my ruby toenails,**
> **Now, I wear jeans with holes that I cut in the knees.**

Once a writer warms up to this type of extension, the poem can take on a life of its own, establishing a rhythm of repeated, back-and-forth lines, alternating between "then" and "now." Poets who extend each line for the sake of special detail can create a magnificent fulcrum at the end with a line or two that breaks the rhythm, either by omitting the extensions, or through a shift of focus.

Repetition

Repetition is probably the oldest structural component of poetry. Before the invention of the printing press, troubadours used rhythm, the repetition of pacing in patterns, and rhyme, the repetition of sound, to help them remember their poems and songs.

Suggesting a specific rhythm often helps writers find words. If someone asks me to write a poem to celebrate an anniversary for someone I hardly know, I can usually do a passable job by taking notes on special details about the persons being honored, then arranging them with the rhythm and simple rhyme scheme of "'Twas the Night Before Christmas." Such a poem almost writes itself!

Repetition is also a rhetorical device, exemplified in great speeches, such as Martin Luther King, Jr.'s "I Have a Dream" speech. Sometimes just the repetition of a key phrase or image, with extensions of image and thought for each repetition, can help a writer generate exciting poems.

Surprise!

All good writing (yes, even term papers) provokes surprise of one kind or another. Many are the ways to keep a reader or listener engaged: a shift of diction, perhaps! Even punctuation can be a surprise. You think this is a sentence. You think this is a sentence! You think this is a sentence! The omission of all punctuation can provide surprise, too:

> **you make me want to throw up**
> **my hands in delight**

A shift in attitude or focus provides other forms of surprise, signaled by a shift in diction:

> **It's delicate when we touch each other ...**

then, ten lines later:

> **I want me one of them riding vacuums!**

(Take a look at the DVD that comes with this book for my performance of "Delicate," from which those lines are quoted.)

A shift in the force of the performer's expression can also work as a surprise, as can the under cutting of a poignant line with the same line spoken more softly, or the same line repeated in the same voice but with a key word or two changed. The list is endless!

Surprise can also come in the delivery of a poem's final lines. I'm interested in the fact that poems with strong, rhythmic endings, perhaps in contrast to many of the preceding lines, score higher than those in which the language has not produced a conclusive rhythm. Given that most judges have little experience with poetry, could one win many a slam with two and a half minutes of gibberish, capped by smart use of thoughtful iambic pentameter in a relatively sensible statement!

> **Thus through all this nonsense you have waded**
> **Let me tell you I am captivated.**

or something like that.

In a reversal of the dictum to "end strong," when I perform my "Introduction," which is

on the accompanying DVD, I attempt to drop all dramatic pretense in the last three lines, lowering my hands and voice as if to shrug. This is the fulcrum, the only moment in the poem where the narrator, a crackpot who believes that time is running backwards, provides a sense of poignancy to all the preceding nonsense:

> **Meanwhile, Presidents and kings are unwaging wars**
> **And back away from their jobs,**
> **Which fall into the laps of those who are ready to retire.**

The jury is still out whether such an anticlimactic, "unique"/"surprise"/"different" way to conclude a slam performance can actually work to advantage.

Attitude

"No attitude, no poem!"

Some students are so beleaguered by the writing of "correct" term papers that they forget that their own feelings and opinions are the stuff of poetry — as are the feelings and opinions of the characters they imagine and in whose voice(s) they write.

I complain about the preponderance of PC poems at poetry slams. My criticism is certainly not that these poems fail to show attitude (heck, they were written for just that purpose), but that the attitude lacks complexity and is indistinguishable from other attitudes that often predominate

at poetry slams. This probably reflects the youth of the poets. I'll bet they also write unique poems, but don't quite trust the audience or, perhaps, themselves: it's risky to stray from what's already succeeded.

So my little crusade is to encourage a unique approach for every slammer. In chapter 6, I suggest that poets conduct an inventory of their physical assets, which may be used to good effect during a performance. What makes you different from others? And how can you use that in a slam poem? Can you create a character who is not you, but has the same unique quality? Someone older, wiser than you perhaps, but wanting to talk about this aspect of difference? Or someone your own age who does not want to talk about it but writes a letter about it? Someone of any age and walk in life who seems unaware of the difference between self and others?

Extending my argument that attitude is everything, I suggest that poets write not what they think they should think and feel, but what they want to think and feel. And about what they do not want to think and feel.

DESIRES
Love
Lust
Success
Money
Fame

FEARS
Death
Public Speaking
Embarrassment
Pain
Assault

These elements of personality fall into two categories: desire and fear. One can create a slam poem that reveals a character's desire or fear. But that's not specific enough, so I'll break down desires into any of the following: Love. Lust. Success. Money. Fame. And for fear I list: Death. Public speaking. Embarrassment. Pain. Assault. Any of these "causes" of attitude can be further expanded, which of course is the job of the poet. So, for example, take "love" from the list of desires: What or who is the object of the love being expressed? In what ways is that "other" of the poem unique? Or, from the list of fears, what is the specific event of "death"? Describing the setting may play an important role in establishing details that contribute to the poem's attitude.

Stuck for a Topic? Read the Newspaper

One of the best places to find topics is the nearest newspaper. Not only does the paper report hundreds of stories each week, but these are often stories with which the reader can identify because the events will affect his or her future, or because they contain "characters" with whom a reader can identify. Events can generate poems of praise or outrage; the characters in a newspaper story can suggest persona, voice, attitude, and/or situation.

Understatement

Just as music in the background of old black-and-white movies tells us how we should feel about each character, how one delivers the lines of a poem captures attitude, so good slammers often write to capture voices they can "hear." Pompous, suspicious, endearing, plaintive – the range of possible voices suggests an enormous variety of personae and topics.

To enhance the humor of an ironic line, try understating it instead of blatantly milking it for its humor. Roger Weingarten, a widely published poet and longtime director of Vermont College's MFA Program in Writing, suggested that I was overplaying a line that wasn't provoking laughs at my readings. "Try it as an aside," he suggested. "Underplay it." So instead of raising my voice, I lowered it at my next reading: The audience laughed! Someday I'll try it as a whisper, and I'll have taken Roger's advice to the edge.

Humor

At the end of my sophomore year in college I gave my first poetry reading. I had saved a short, sad poem for the end. It's called "Seasons." I was surprised when the audience laughed:

> Today you remove it from the freezer,
>
> and the snowball you have saved since March
>
> misses the ice cream truck entirely.

In fact, my feelings were a little hurt that people could laugh at such a sad event. But after the reading, I realized that this was the only time in the entire half-hour that I could remember the audience laughing.

Uh-oh.

In a slam, the poet has only three minutes, not a whole half-hour, so it's understandable that humor may not be part of the poem. But if there's a chance that a line can be delivered in a way that offers the audience a chance to smile or laugh, go for it. I'm lucky to have learned so early that an audience needs a chance to identify with the poet, and humor – perhaps unplanned or even unintended – provides the quickest link to the audience's empathy. Wit and subtle characterization work best; clowning usually becomes tiresome, though some students will want to experiment with it.

The Pause

Just as an audience's laughter can surprise the poet, and just as the poet can also plan for laughter, the pause is useful for both unexpected as well as planned moments. For me at least, it's harder to sustain a planned pause than one occasioned by an unexpected event. As unhurriedly as I try to perform my work, I inevitably feel the urge to get to the end as quickly as possible. I'm trained not to waste an audience's time, and poetry, with its emphasis on compact language, encourages respect for the audience's time. Pausing for effect during the delivery of a poem violates instinct and contradicts the notion of efficient delivery of language and feeling. Yet the pause provides a sense of drama that words alone cannot.

The pause also has an important effect at the beginning of a performance. Inexperienced slammers often start to read or recite their poems before the audience is ready. I've even seen performers who begin speaking before they've taken their place onstage. I had the habit of rushing into performances too, until my actor friend Donny Osman told me to take the time to "gather the energy of the audience" before speaking. Although these four or five seconds can seem like eternity to the anxious performer, they provide the opportunity to scan the audience, maybe smile at a familiar face, and wait for room noise to fall to the perfect "expectant hush." Such composed silence is created by the performer's composure, which suggests confidence and earns an attentive audience for a poem's all-important first lines.

A stanza break in a poem implies a pause, but even poems without stanza breaks offer these opportunities. Think of the intentional pause as a fresh chance to "gather the energy" of the audience. Sudden silence from the stage – an interruption in the flow of words – creates surprise and alerts the audience that something new is about to happen. I have to struggle to hold such a pause to the point where the audience verges on becoming uncomfortable – all of three or four seconds – but that's my goal. An almost palpable sense of relief, the equivalent of a noiseless group sigh, permeates the room as the performance continues. If the placement of such a pause is strategically plotted, the audience will have a moment to reflect on the words that have already been delivered, and perhaps an instant of Has-the-poet-lost-it! uncertainty before the positive settling of doubts with the resumption of speech.

Of course, a poem's fulcrum is one of the best places to pause, especially when it occurs toward the end of the poem, where some resolution or reflection will occur. This pause represents the unspoken, lawyerly "Therefore..."

The Unplanned Pause

There's that terrible moment, once every thirty or forty performances, when an audience is with you, then suddenly every head in the room swivels 180 degrees to view an usher on a ladder who, replacing a light bulb unobtrusively, collapses and who is now unconscious, draped over the ladder, and they're getting a doctor as your voice stutters to realization.

My instinct is to raise my voice, to conquer the distraction, but in such horrible circumstances, of course, it never works. "The show must go on" perhaps, but good slamming requires grace in dire situations and, I believe, more often honors silence than blathering.

Of course I've presented an extreme case, but consider those less dire and more frequent moments when something goes wrong. For instance, **you lose your place in the poem you are reading or reciting: What do you do?**

> **1. You apologize and/or start over;**
>
> **2. You keep talking even though you have no idea where it's all leading;**
>
> **3. You shut up for however long it takes to figure out what should happen next.**

Choose number three! Your audience will think it was all part of the act, the pause having created a sense of urgency and, perhaps, concern. But never letting on that the pause itself was covering a moment of confusion will, nine times out of ten, carry the day.

Starting Points for Writing: A Writing Race

I am a speed writer. Writing as fast as I can helps me find rhythms, the words tumbling onto the page faster than I can think of them. Because it works for me, I impose speed writing on everyone in the classroom. Third graders, high school students, adults – everyone faces the same opening challenge to "write as fast as you can, nonstop, for seven minutes. **"Pencils up!"** (Here I pause to ensure that everyone, myself included, is holding pencil or pen high above the head.) **"Get set!** **Spelling and neatness don't count, as long as you can read the writing; the answer to any question you may have is what you want it to be; prize goes to the longest piece ... Write!"**

Upon that final command, I plunge my pen to my notebook and begin seven to ten minutes of furious scribbling. Who knows what will appear on the page?

It's a writing race if you will, a good way to clear the mind of self-doubt even as one lowers expectations, perhaps only hoping for something from which may be salvaged two or three bits of good fortune. But sometimes, just sometimes, the rhythm of the activity brings forth entire poems or stories deserving of admiration. The variables here may well be the luck of the writing prompt and what the individual writer ate for breakfast.

A brief word of warning: Students reading their freshly written poems may speed their reading of the work because they have just engaged in a writing race. If you ask students to read their fresh poems, be sure to explain the need to shift gears!

As with all writing, there's wisdom in caring enough for poems thus generated to revise them. This can be a tough sell to young writers, and I'm quick to tell them that I bother to revise only those entries in my notebook that seem worth the effort, which is about five percent.

Writing to Fill

Although I contend that there is no such thing as a "slam poem," certain structural components lend themselves to successful performance. Repetition and humor are two useful strategies, used independently or together. Compare-and-contrast strategies also work well, as long as the audience doesn't sense the setup and begin to anticipate the forthcoming contrast.

Structural frameworks work wonders in forcing the issue with blocked writers; in fact I often impose them on myself. Again, if it works for me, it'll probably work in the classroom, so I often challenge students to fulfill the demands of one arbitrarily chosen structure or another. Structures certainly include the traditional existing forms, including the sonnet, limerick, haiku, and so forth. But what about other structures, those without formal names?

Poems written to fulfill an arbitrary structural demand often benefit, during revision, from the deletion of some or all of the structural elements that led to the poem's generation.

Parody and Other Forms of Imitation

One can deduce an infinite variety of writing strategies simply by analyzing a variety of poems, possibly borrowing as many of these strategies as desired. Borrow too many, as in my willful use of the meter and rhyme scheme of "'Twas the Night Before Christmas," and the resulting poem may be perceived as parody. But many contemporary poems can lend strategies without the source's becoming quite so obvious.

Here's **"Passing Thru,"** as performed on the accompanying DVD:

You see them at truckstops, signs that litter the walls:
Work Fascinates Me, I Can Sit & Watch it for Hours, Plan Ahea
And the waitress so sullen you want to tip extra just to show her
How wrong she was about you, her white dress with little bumps
All over the material making it look almost gray and you see thru
To the bra doing its thin job and she wants you to pay up
So she can go home, saunters over and yawns between chews, "Youthru?"
And not to be mean but because you're lonely you ask for another donut:
She extends it with aluminum pincers so it seems germproof,
But you watched earlier as she emptied the bakery cellophane damn near
Fondling each one as if here at least was something she cared for
And licking all the extra sugar off her fingers at the end.

"To hell with aluminum—let's dance!" you cry and twist her hand
Over the counter so she drops pincers and your donut
"Hey cut that out, whatsa matter with you you crazy or somethin: Joe!"
And she starts yelling but you've already passed thru
That critical tunnel where you decide:
"This is a dream, I'll do what I please"
And one of the truckers looks up from the coffee he stirred with his eyes
As you think of your mother who told you about them
And how one would kill you someday just like they got your father

PAGE
52

And you dance with her back and forth over the countertop
Until Joe comes out at which point the trucker gets involved too
And both of them have you by the legs and the waitress is saying
"Wise guy wise guy" over and over
And the pincers and your donut are on the floor
And if you wanna know more go do it yourself

Structural elements one might borrow from "Passing Thru" include: Starting with the first line, the poem is cast in the second person, probably first person in disguise. The narrator is using the "royal you," which implies his experience thrust upon the reader. This use of the second person has a slightly menacing quality, and goes a long way toward establishing attitude. To observe the differences in tone among first, second, and third person, try rereading the poem in the first person, then try the third person.

The first line also suggests an object or objects, perhaps the topic of the poem, but mysterious, vague: "them." This evokes curiosity, so the reader continues to the second line, where the mystery is solved. In the third line, the narrator elaborates with specific citation, direct quotes from the signs, and the reader gains more familiarity with the setting.

Perhaps this almost predictable setting causes depression. For whatever reason, the character who is introduced in the next line seems to match the setting, not just because she's a waitress. Elaboration on her costume resonates with the setting and increases the reader's familiarity with the scene.

Continuing to analyze the poem's structure, we see that it's basically a straight, chronological narrative in which events are linked by "and," and drama is created through colloquial dialogue, all cast in the universal second person, present tense. In addition to changing the person of the poem while rereading it, one might also experiment with the effect of shifting the verb tense. Notice how moving the poem from present to past tense saps its intensity! But think of the difference this kind of shift can make in other poems – sometimes a positive difference. Encourage students to experiment with such revisions in their own poems!

Another way to borrow strategy is to plot the specific bones of observed structure, and simply "write to fill." For this activity, it might be best not to show students the complete poem, but just ask them to work with the bare bones. For **"Passing Thru,"** one might provide:

You see them ..."

and ..."

and ..."

and ..."

Hey, ..."
"What's the ...!"

and ...
and if you wanna .....

Five Exercises for Slam Poets

Here are some of my favorite exercises. They offer an unusual number of opportunities to include the special elements of a successful slam poem.

I am from ... where the phrase "I am from" repeats as many times as the author finds appropriate. Consider shifting the persona of the speaker, or the specific "place" with each repetition of that key phrase. I learned this powerful exercise from a piece George Ella Lyon published in Potato Hill Poetry's lively, but, alas, late and deeply missed newsletter.

A sappy love poem ... Often this evokes rhymed iambic pentameter or silly limericks: that's fine. The point here is to specify "sappy" so the writers stretch in a direction opposite the high quality for which they may have habitually been striving. Relieving expectation offers a kind of freedom that sometimes results in a better poem than would have occurred under the stress of attempting something grand. This writing activity might even lead to a "Sappy Love Poem Slam," where audiences and judges value most highly the most saccharine.

Discover Writing Press   www.discoverwriting.com   © 2005

A haiku race ... In this activity, students compose as many haiku as they can in seven minutes. With luck, some participants will stumble into the rhythm of haiku and cease to need to count syllables. For some writers, thinking of the tune to **"Moonlight in Vermont"** can guide this process:

**Pennies in a stream,
Falling leaves of sycamore,
Moonlight in Vermont.**

After seven minutes, glancing confidently at my collection of seven or eight haiku, each comprising seventeen syllables of nonsense, I ask, "Has anyone written three or more?" As many as eighty percent of the students will raise their hands. "How about five or more!"

And so on, until only one hand remains. Or we can stage a haiku race showdown in a number of ways, perhaps each of us reading a haiku in turn, going around the classroom, then again and again until only one or two of us have a haiku left to read: the winners! Each of us might also present all our haiku in single performances, linking them together as one might perform separate stanzas of a poem.

A recipe poem ... where poets use the imperative mood. It helps to provide examples of the imperative mood, showing a variety of attitudes, from "Give me the money," as spoken by a bank robber armed with a loaded pistol, to "Give me the grace to be kind to my neighbor," as spoken in prayer. Recipe poems offer a chance for student writers to explore persona: perhaps the voice of the poem can be a parent giving a series of commands to a child or a demanding boss instructing her subordinate. It might be someone who is providing directions: "Take a left at the house of pain ..." Indeed, it might be the voice of a cookbook: "Add a pinch of love, and stir like crazy."

A collaborative poem ... written before anyone but the teacher knows that a "poem" is the goal of the exercise. Give participants twenty-two seconds to "write a phrase, just a phrase"

PAGE
55

(this usually requires a brief review of grammatical jargon), "something you observed between waking and arriving at this room." I'm always careful to use the verb "observed" instead of "saw," because "observed" suggests a broader range of sensual responses than "saw." "Pencils up: Get set: Write!" After twenty-two seconds, the time it takes me to enter a phrase into my notebook, I call on students at random to read their phrases, which I write, word for word, on the board. When someone prefaces his or her phrase with "I wrote …" I interrupt: "Don't describe what you wrote, just read the words off the paper. Just the words." I jump at the chance to mis-interpret a homonym or other type of word that I can scramble, writing "bare" for "bear," "widow" for "window," and "unclear" instead of "nuclear." This generates focused scrutiny from the group; students delight in catching a teacher's mistakes! Additionally, I feel free to ask about punctuation, adding commas and exclamation points, question marks, et cetera, exactly as they appear in the student's original phrase.

Once no room remains on the board, sometimes after I've interjected my own twenty-two-second phrase, I say, "That's enough. Now let's see what we've got." I take a step back from the board and read the first line aloud slowly and with feeling, continuing to the second line and onward, sometimes vocally implying an exclamation point or a long pause, sometimes running lines together to create meaning that no contributor intended. When I get to the final line, I slow down further, giving as much emphasis as possible to whatever rhythm might turn up. "Now," I ask, "what have we here!"

"A poem!"

"Yes, but why is it a poem!"

"Well, it paints a kind of picture."

"And the way you read it – you made it sound like a poem!"

These are the answers I've been hoping to hear. They provide the definition of a good "slam poem." The exercise has created images, and the results can be performed in a way that distinguishes the work from prose. It matters less what the words say, perhaps, than how the piece sounds. A performer who observes a few common conventions of public presentation can sell even a string of randomly chosen phrases as a poem.

If I am composing with only a slam audience in mind, I want to write a good poem that has built-in opportunities for gesture, for hissing, possibly for silence, maybe for my own laughter or other variations of my speaking voice. If I'm composing with only a slam audience in mind, I want to write for the stage!

Memorizing Versus Learning by Heart

Elizabeth Thomas is a miracle slam teacher who organizes and hosts youth slams in Connecticut and each spring drives a carload of students to Brave New Voices. She tells her students, "If you know your poem really well, your performance will follow."

Poets who recite their poems without a manuscript in hand usually earn higher scores than those who need to read their work. Naturally, they have greater opportunity to make meaningful eye contact with members of the audience, just as, because their hands are free, they have greater freedom to gesture.

A few years ago, I attended a presentation of original poems by Cora Brooks at the public library in Chelsea, Vermont. She performed for nearly an hour, standing in front of her audience and offering poem after poem without once referring to a manuscript. At the reception afterward, I asked Brooks what tricks she used to memorize her work.

"I don't memorize," she replied. "I learn my poems by heart."

This distinction has made a big difference in my ability to perform "off book." For me, at least, the semantic difference between **memorize**, struggling to imprint the brain with a discrete sequence of many, many words, and **learn by heart** mirrors the difference between painful, perfectionist mental struggle and the ease of carrying the spirit of a poem within, so that the work is always accessible, even when the performer has momentarily lost his or her place.

PAGE
57

Chapter 6: Eyes & Voice: Classroom Exercises/Coaching

When I first meet with a group of potential slammers, I often tell them that I'm going to slam my favorite poem, and that they should take notes on how I might improve my performance. I then rush to the "stage," manuscript in hand, already speaking before I reach my place. At various moments during my reading, I hold the manuscript in front of my face, mumble, drop my voice to less than an audible whisper, refuse to make eye contact, tap my foot or pace without purpose, scratch, and indulge in other gestures that have no relationship to the words of my poem.

Students seem to enjoy telling me the many things I've done wrong. The demonstration helps to embed in their minds all the "sins" of bad slamming; it also suggests that even a teacher can gracefully accept constructive criticism. As they discuss the ways in which I can improve my performance, I remain silent, just listening and taking notes. I want the students to learn this difficult skill: to hear what others have to say, and take the feedback seriously enough to write down their suggestions. Above all, I don't waste the group's time by responding defensively, as in, "I was trying to show how a shy child with hives might read this poem, which is why I scratched." Instead, I respond, and only briefly, after all comments have been offered. I encourage the students to do the same.

Revision

I am careful to remind students that they alone are the owners of the poem, and they need accept only those suggestions that they think will lead to an improved presentation. Same goes for suggestions regarding the content of the poem. Revision generally does not work when the writer's heart is not in considering alternatives and making the changes.

It probably goes without saying that many students, especially teenagers, are reluctant to

revise their poems. When I tell a group how much I love to revise, eyes roll and smirks appear. Is this because many students equate revision to editing? In any case, revision is necessary, I explain, in almost every poem I like enough to want to take to a slam.

What do I look for when it's time to revise? First of all, I check continuity and context. Does the poem make sense? Will the listener know when, where, and how the events in the poem have occurred? Second, I go on an adjective and adverb hunt, checking to be sure that those modifiers are truly needed. More often than not, I can delete the modifier by finding a strong synonym for the word being modified. Failing that, I can introduce metaphor or simile, again as compensation for the deleted modifiers. My goal is to reduce by at least fifty percent the number of adjectives and adverbs in the poem. Needless to say, this sort of revision is just as creative as the act of composition, and students who try it (only on the drafts they think show promise) often find that their attitude toward revision changes.

Eyes

I know two or three excellent musicians who, for some reason, keep their eyes shut the whole time they sing. I love their CDs but avoid their concerts. It may be that voice and content are the two most important elements of successful performance, but eye contact comes in a powerful third. I don't want to fake it, either, by accepting the bad advice of theater experts – "Focus over the heads of your audience toward the back wall" – or by timidly glimpsing only a brief snapshot of any audience member's face. I call this "token eye contact."

Instead, I want to form memorable images of my audience, which means allowing my eyes to linger on five or six people, in different places, as I perform. "Giving" the poem to this randomly selected core group provides a secondary but essential element, a reading on how well the poem is being accepted. If someone refuses to return eye contact or is yawning, I'm probably in trouble!

Performing with Manuscript: Read, Lift, and Give

For the slammer who needs to hold a manuscript, some simple advice:

Discover Writing Press   www.discoverwriting.com   © 2005

1. Whenever possible, have the entire poem on a single sheet of paper, using both sides if necessary.

2. If the poem requires more than one sheet of paper, use only one side of each page, number the pages, and, in performance, slide "used" pages unobtrusively from top to bottom; do not allow them to flutter to the floor, which, however dramatic the intended effect, distracts the audience.

3. Hold the manuscript as low as possible, away from your face.

4. If you have to read the poem line by line, use the "read, lift, and give" method for establishing meaningful eye contact: read the line silently, lift it from the page, and with eyes and voice give it to a member of the audience, then read aloud a line or two directly from the page before reading, lifting, and giving again. Varying the sequence and rhythm of these operations will prevent their becoming predictable.

5. Print the manuscript in as large a font as necessary to be able to read it when it's laid on the floor of the stage.

Eye Contact Exercises

1. Stand in front of the group and look into the eyes of one member of the audience. Say, with deep sincerity, "I am a duck, zigging and zagging across a pond of rippling water."

2. Repeat the above, but establish eye contact with two members of your audience: half the line for one person, the other half for another audience member.

3. Take a poem from your notebook that you have not yet performed and "read, lift, and give" it to your audience.

4. Learn a poem by heart and perform it with lighting that prevents your seeing the audience. Ask members of the audience whether you established meaningful eye contact or just seemed to be blinking in the dark.

5. Rehearse under as wide a variety of audience and lighting conditions as possible. Scatter the audience around the room and try "reading" the expressions of members under the glare of a spotlight; try it again with house lights up full.

Voice

Of course there's "the voice" of the poem, but here I am specifically addressing the noise-making instrument of the performer. A few of us have resonant voices, what might be called "good pipes," so that projection and reception of sound are effortless for performer and audience, respectively. But the majority of us, myself included, are less generously endowed.

In my case, whenever I hear a recording of my spoken efforts, I am chagrined by the raspy near-whine emanating from the stranger who is performing a poor imitation of what I'm hearing when I open my mouth. I suppose the best hope for me, a tenor with enthusiasm but weak pipes, would be to waken from a long sleep half an hour before the performance and not use my voice until I took the stage. Or to have slams scheduled for whenever I'm "suffering" with a cold that has deepened my voice.

My friend Jim DeFilippi, teacher, mystery novelist, and successful comic, once made the uninvited suggestion that I growl before each performance, finding the lowest possible sound I can make. This confirmed my worst self-doubts: Hewitt, you ain't got the pipes. But it gave me a tool for overcoming my limitation. Another friend, Michael Nedell, has suggested that I sing as a way to keep my voice in shape.

Voice Exercises

For those who want to warm up before performances, here are five exercises that I've used with good effect.

1. Find the lowest note you can sing by starting a scale and moving down from the starting point. Push yourself to get a half note or a quarter note lower, until all you can make is a grunting sound. Hum that note as an "om" for five minutes, inhaling only as necessary. (Do not do this while driving!) After five minutes, attempt to lower the tone by another half- or quarter note, and repeat the exercise. Do this until you have reached the very bottom of your audible scale.

2. Explore your upper range by singing a scale upward, finding your falsetto range, a place in the upper register where you'll feel your voice "break" into a more screechy sound,

sometimes called "head voice." This sound comes from a different place in the body than your regular voice. Some people also have a "throat voice," the low-range equivalent of falsetto, a clearly projectable bass rumble that I've heard Peter Schumann, founder of Bread and Puppet Theater, deliver with conviction.

The point of these first two exercises is to experience your body as a producer of extremes, so in a room where no one can hear you (a parked car with the windows rolled up will do), explore the edges of your highest and lowest notes. As you do this, experiment with your breathing – from gentle, lengthy inhaling to choppy, stomach pumping exhalation – to influence the sound. Make yourself a human accordion, issuing the sounds as if someone were punching your belly five times a second.

3. Think about your quiet voice. How will you establish emotional range in a performance? Are there moments when your persona might actually hiss? Or whisper? Or pause to underscore a perfect irony? Okay, that last suggestion relates to timing, and of course there's a marvelous and mysterious field of response that can be mined by the artful uses of voice in concert with timing. The poem's shape on the page might offer some clues.

4. Experiment with breathing. Discover how many words you can say in a single breath. Practice deep breathing, and learn where, in your poems, a long string of words should go uninterrupted by unnecessary inhalation, and, conversely, where the act of inhaling might provide dramatic emphasis.

5. A comedian I met on an airplane told me he writes out his routines as poems, the line breaks generally suggesting how he should time the delivery of his patter. To explore the possibilities of timing, write a poem where the lines, in couplets, ask a question in line

one and provide an answer in line two. Take that poem onstage and find a variety of voices that can emanate among the shifting personae of the questioners and the responders. Where humor is possible through gesture or pause or change in facial expression, explore what you can do, experimenting with my three-line poem, "Afterthought":

> "Will she ever set the world on fire? No,"
>
> Mr. Evans, Guidance, asked and answered, kindly.
>
> Perhaps she should be President!

Ignoring punctuation, experiment with how many different ways those lines can be spoken. Consider the various inflections and tones of voice for the first line, perhaps in contrast to the narrator's voice in lines two and three. Pause after each line so each line solidifies into its own statement, then run the lines together and let the meaning follow the punctuation.

Guarding Enthusiasm

To every poem I perform I bring a guarded enthusiasm, some level of identity with the voice of the poem, and a studied commitment to the audience's apprehending each word. When I think of my positive qualities, the first that come to mind are my awareness of how easily words are misheard and a lifetime's experience playing on the page with potential ambiguities, depending on homonyms, punctuation, and emphasis, perhaps conveyed by rhythm. What better place than slam to provide resolution to those ambiguities!

But my insistence on articulating each word precisely may have a negative effect, seeming too precious. How much to trust the audience beyond giving a performance that resembles a good-hearted librarian's reading of picture books to squirming three-year-olds?

When I mention my "guarded enthusiasm," I acknowledge that as soon as I start to perform the poem, I forget all the growling potential of my voice and enter the persona of the poem. Because I wrote the poem, I can usually assume a persona without too much fishing around. But I recognize my own potential for goofiness, especially if encouraged by a lively crowd, so I know the horror of having gone too far, having allowed myself to enjoy the crowd's admiration too much, spoiling the performance. The slam equivalent of the dictum "Don't laugh at your own jokes" is this advice: Don't let on that you're aware of the audience's appreciation; don't oversell your poem; just stay within the range of its persona. Getting carried away with the brilliance of the moment shines a blinding signal to the audience which, suddenly aware of the poet's glowing, is no longer following the words.

An Eight-Day Curriculum to Build Confident Slammers

First Day: Take an honest inventory of your body.

Long arms? Great! Beer belly or other significant shape in profile? Terrific! Feet splayed like a duck's? You can use that. What about your head or hair or face, the double-jointed shoulder you can use as part of the character(s) you're building for a public performance of three minutes? **Remember: your voice and your body are your only props.**

Next item for inventory is your voice. How big is it? Can you project anger without screaming? Can you whisper audibly or sing like a meadowlark? My bet is that singer/ composers could clean up at slams, yet only twice in the four years I've been slamming have I heard someone perform an original song.

Equally important to noting the qualities and capabilities of your voice is knowing the circumstances in which it best serves you, and how you can best re-create those circumstances. Students with quiet speaking voices often have excellent vocal projection when calling to a friend across the street. A good starting point is to write a poem where the voice of the poem is that of someone calling to a friend across the street. Of course, then you should deliver it that way, hands cupped around the mouth, megaphone-style!

Once the inventory of body and voice is complete, write a short poem that uses some of your "advantages." Long arms? Write a poem that invites the audience to imagine the outstretched wings of a hawk, and, in performance, show those wings.

PAGE
65

Homework for Day Two: Substitute "duh" or "hud" for each syllable of your poem, experimenting with the rhythms you find and the differences in rhythms among words that have the same number of syllables. For example, compare "experiment" to "reestablish." Rehearse the piece, speaking only "duh" or "hud" for each syllable. Explore the inventory of movement, expression, and voice you established during day one. Experiment with the rhythms possible when you string five or six monosyllables together.

The trick to this exercise lies in repeating it. Rehearse it enough as homework so you are ready to perform the same piece twice in virtually identical performances. It's probably best to write it out as a score, possibly with annotations for gesture, expression, and movement. Use your score when you perform:

HUD - HUD - HUD - DUH
HUD - DUH - DUH - DUH
HUD - DUH - HUD - HUD - DUH ?

Hud-hud, hud-hud, duh, hud
[shrugging]   [hands on hips]
Duh duh duh duh duh duh
[one step toward audience, rising voice]

Perform the piece again, this time imagining a question mark at the end of each line.

Activity for Day Two: A typical first response to this exercise, coming just as the group's members are getting to know each other, is embarrassment. Participants may simply try to ease themselves off stage with a limerick, shrugging or giggling at the end. This is normal human behavior in the course of a silly exercise, but do not allow such performances to be all that a participant offers. Encourage repetition of a performance until the slammer can do it without conveying

Discover Writing Press   www.discoverwriting.com   © 2005

embarrassment. Be patient, but do not force the issue with any student who is not making progress. This is not punishment; it's simply reinforcing a notion of control in performance, and given time it comes, usually in a day or two. "Confidence. Conviction. Do it again and show these qualities."

Homework for Day Three: Rehearse your poem again, this time with the original words **and** using "duh" or "hud" for each syllable.

Activity for Day Three: Perform both versions of your poem, and take notes on the group's suggestions for improved performance. Explore these suggestions by performing the piece one last time.

Homework for Day Four: Slammers search the library or a bookstore for a poem by someone else, to perform in three minutes or less. They are encouraged to review their inventories and reflect on what they learned from the performances of "Duh," using all the tools they can draw into the performance. At this point, they may be gaining an awareness of their "style."

A useful discussion, as the group addresses these "cover" performances, is how group members would describe one another's emerging style. In cases where no description of style is forthcoming, it's sometimes useful to ask how a style might be created. Is this a reticent person or a screamer? How can one build on these characteristics?

Activity for Day Four: Students perform and discuss their cover poems.

Homework for Day Five: Take your cover poem to the edge. Either exaggerate your "style" to the point where it becomes self-mockery, or use a suggestion from day four as the direction you'll take the poem, all the way to the edge.

So if someone has suggested that you speak some of the declarative sentences as if they ended with question marks, perform each line as a question, just to explore the effect. If someone suggests that you not wobble from foot to foot, rehearse the poem as if you are the trunk of a giant

oak on a day with no wind. If your style is described as somber, try for maudlin; if your style is labeled "lively," experiment with antic.

Activity for Day Five: Perform your cover poem by taking it to the edge. Provide time for a group discussion after each performance.

Homework for Day Six: Rehearse the same poem, but this time going for exactly the opposite of day five's performance. The antic performer becomes the trunk of a giant oak, the maudlin delivery becomes uplifting or at least deadpan, the question marks are replaced by exclamation points.

Activity for Day Six: Perform the cover poem, as rehearsed, taking it in the opposite direction from day five. Hold a group discussion after each performance.

Homework for Day Seven: Write your own slam poem, calling on all the elements you've explored since your first day's inventory. What have you learned about your style upon which a poem of your own can now build? Or, just for the fun of it (and to win the first slam, which is the day after tomorrow, day eight), you might explore the element of surprise by giving your audience exactly the opposite of what they expect of you!

Activity for Day Seven: Pair up and ask your partner to read your poem, using all possible gestures from your inventory. Offer a critique, then ask your partner to repeat the performance. The person whose poem is being rehearsed acts as director and, after fifteen minutes of working in pairs, the students perform their partners' poems to the whole class.

Homework for Day Eight: Rehearse in preparation for the slam.

Activity for Day Eight: Slam!

For the Rest of the Semester: The eight-day sequence can be repeated, possibly omitting the first inventories and perhaps the "duh" exercises. But, as a means of encouraging active reading on the part of the slammers, continue the "cover slams," which will push participants to discover capabilities they might not realize through their own poems, presumably composed with only their known skills in mind.

Variations on the cover slam include assigning specific poems to specific students (you can find hundreds of fine slam poems in the books listed in the Appendix, "The Best Slam Resources"). Or participants can all rehearse and perform the same poem, a fascinating exercise that reveals the chosen poem's depth, and provides an amazing dynamic of observation and attempted differentiation in the actual performances.

After one or two cycles, some students will want to take slam out of the classroom, which should be a goal of any group leader – encourage the discipline as a part of "real life." Depending on personalities and available venues, it's best to provide some initial support, then to withdraw from the **organizing** work. Believe me, the events will be better and will have some chance of longevity if they belong to the participants, not the group leader. On the other hand, a good group leader will attend the slams and, as often as possible, compete for the cash prizes!

Encouraging "Shy" and Reluctant Students to Slam

I rarely encounter reluctance in elementary-level classrooms, but starting at seventh grade, some students shy away from slamming, at times even refusing to recite or peform their poems. Recently I've noticed that if I expect every student to participate, every student does, although some, admittedly, perform with less enthusiasm than others. Perhaps my "expectation" comes across to students as a requirement; this is fine by me, unless it seems to be creating an unhealthy level of stress. Elizabeth Thomas suggests that reluctant students be offered the option of creating team poems, where as many as four poets write and perform a collaborative piece.

See the accompanying DVD for examples.

SLAM IN THE WORLD
Chapter 7: Slam Outside the Classroom

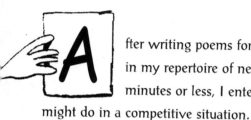

After writing poems for forty years, I feel that I have an edge in most slams. Secure in my repertoire of nearly two hundred solid poems that I can recite or read in three minutes or less, I enter slams gladly, curious to see how such and such a poem might do in a competitive situation.

But also curious to see whether I can pull it off. I've got the content down, I'm convinced, but can my reading or recitation of a poem recapture the assuredness I felt when I was composing it? Can I recapture the spontaneity of the moment when the words first appeared? Can I enter that moment, the mood of the poem? Will I catch, in my reading, the rhythmic shifts that a careless reader would surely miss? In some poems, the meaning comes through only when the rhythms are emphasized, then undercut by a drifting monotone so the words can best speak for themselves.

"Understatement." That was Roger Weingarten's advice, and he was right.

Slam Strategy: The Right Poem at the Right Moment

Most slams offer two or three rounds, with the lowest-scoring poets eliminated at the end of each round. My strategy is generally to survive the early rounds and to wow 'em in the final round. But different slams use different procedures, and in slams where scores are cumulative, one might consider performing the strongest work first, thus avoiding elimination and earning a high enough score to buoy ensuing offerings. Of course a lot depends on the judges: if they seem to be tiring of bombast, I offer a poem that offers sweetness and forgiveness. If the judges have been most favorably disposed toward outrageous performances, I'll perform a poem that exceeds my normal range of outrage.

"The right poem at the right moment" is the driving force behind selections, which argues for the preparation of several choices for a slam. Even if "the right poem" means that I have to

read the poem, eschewing my preference for the poems that I know by heart, I'll attempt to "lift" the unfamiliar words from the page, pausing between lines, to "give" the poem's lines to each member of the audience with my eyes. This may slow the delivery, but this can be an advantage: after all, those words are unfamiliar to the audience and, heck, it's a poem that deserves to be understood!

Sometimes a poem that seems stale to me, too often slammed, is "the right poem" for the moment. One can perform the tried and true, especially given an audience that encompasses a few well-placed pals just dying for the humorous denouement.

Score Creep, Luck, and Other Phenomena

There are lots of reasons to hope for a high number in the sequence of slammers drawn from the proverbial hat. The first is score creep, an immeasurable but provable phenomenon (if that's not a paradox, what is!) wherein no matter how thoroughly the slammaster has instructed the judges to score each performance relative to the sacrificial poet's, scores tend to rise throughout a bout. So a high number offers the obvious benefit of score creep. It also affords the optimum opportunity for strategizing.

The higher your number in the draw, the more you can strategize, observing judges' biases and assessing what kind of poem and performance are most likely to strike it rich. With a high draw, one can gauge whether the all-out, go-for-broke effort of a best poem is needed, or whether that poem can be held in reserve.

But it goes without saying that you need a strategy for the unpleasant possibility of an early draw. If you're going to be among the first twenty-five percent or so of the slammers, you need to use up your best poem simply to offset the effects of score creep. You'll never make it into the second round with anything less than your best if you are first in the draw, and subtract one or two percent from your "best" for each slot thereafter within the first half. If in a twelve-slot slam, you are the seventh slammer or later, you'll have the likely benefit of score creep plus enough vantage on what has already transpired to select from your full range of works.

Strategy from a Master

Anyone looking for strong team strategies should consult Taylor Mali's authoritative guide to winning at the Nationals, **Top Secret Slam Strategies**. One of Mali's chief themes is that team spirit is what counts, not the individual drive that got you onto the team in the first place. Check your ego at the door.

Mali's helpful booklet also analyzes the consequences of exceeding the time limit. He offers mathematical projections that demonstrate why a poet who is heading into overtime will score higher with an abrupt ending than with the completed poem earning its due score, then receiving a time penalty. He suggests that a signal from a team member be arranged at the 2:30 mark, by which time the poet should be at or beyond a point where the rest of the poem can be comfortably completed within the remaining thirty seconds. A predetermined escape route to quicker completion will help the lagging poet to avert panic and perhaps prevent the audience's realizing the omission of several precious but potentially costly lines.

The Beauties of Preparation

Of course the key to all slams is careful preparation. Nothing feels better than entering a slam with six or eight solid poems under your belt, poems that can unquestionably be performed in three minutes or less. This element of planning, often overlooked, allows for strategy decisions as the event unfolds. For instance, knowing one's sequence in a given round – whether performing among the first three poets or in the middle of the pack or last of all – makes a difference in whether to perform a political rant or a graceful sonnet. Generally, early slots should be approached with a lively performance, ideally one that evokes laughter and helps the audience find comfort and delight. Later in the round, a poet might instead choose to perform a more thoughtful poem, especially if antic performances have dominated the early slots. The later one is in the sequence, the greater the opportunity to observe the judges' biases and to gauge whether a certain type of performance has already been overdone.

If hip-hop poets dominate the evening, I'll choose unrhyming poems where the rhythms are not regular, attempting to establish my performance as different from all the others. In whatever

PAGE
73

way I can convince myself a certain poem is "different," I'll go with that poem nine times out of ten. I figure I have a fifty-percent chance of victory if I can be different from all the other performers.

Anything Goes, But ...

In slam, anything goes. Extreme ideas and harsh language may not win big points, but slam is first and foremost loyal to the precepts of free speech. Honestly, I have never been offended at a slam, except by the piles of politically correct rant that takes no risk at all, but which, performed skillfully, wows the neophyte judges. It seems that all poets are in favor of peace and equality, with a sense of justice that should be extended, and sometimes demonstrably so, to all beings, regardless of ethnicity, religion, color, gender, marital status, or sexual preference. For me, the poems declaring outrage at oppression and poems that express other outright PC beliefs are almost always the equivalent of someone's saying "I'm glad to breathe fresh air" or "grass is generally green in color." Hello?

Yet, I admit to performing such poems when no previous competitor has offered them – a rare circumstance. When are people going to start listening at slams for fresh ideas, sharp, physical, sensual imagery, inventive language? When these elements are in place, one probably has a true poem. The problem then becomes how to perform it. The poem of PC outrage merely requires a voice quivering with passion and an occasional outstretched fist. So easy. And, I'll add, so cheap. Is it the stereotyping of slam as an activity where foul language, predictable rhymes, yelling, and political rant prevail that prevents broader participation by most of our book-published poets, whose work on the page suggests poetry as higher art?

These poets may also be uneasy in a competitive situation where performance skills can dominate. Maybe it takes a special arrogance to slam, trotting one's most sensitive insights before a crowd of people who may or may not know anything about poetry.

But that is also the charm and the first precept of slam: it is of the people and for the people, regardless how insensitive, rowdy, or drunk they may be. A good slammer can read the crowd and the judges, choosing poems appropriately. Again, there's incentive here to build a repertoire, writing and rehearsing a variety of poems, poems fit for any occasion. Knowing that audiences vary from respectful, supportive, or reserved, to unconscious, stoned, uninterested, or

Discover Writing Press   www.discoverwriting.com   © 2005

raucous, and knowing that an audience might go through any or all these phases in stages as the event progresses, a good slammer considers these possibilities in preparing.

The Mysterious Stranger

It helps to know the venue. But there's no thrill like discovering in the alternative newspaper a slam scheduled on the very night you are idle in a strange city, sleeping over in a cheap motel.

Swaggering into the sunset with your book bag bulging with manuscripts and copies of your book for sale, you are hopeful, even optimistic. You find the bus stop almost effortlessly, and enjoy the bumpy ride across town to a small bar in a seedy district near a couple of housing developments, just downhill from the college. I guess it's a poet's equivalent to John Wayne's busting through the swinging doors of a North Dakota tavern before the Great Depression, approaching the slammaster as a mysterious stranger and signing up for the evening's festivities.

I've done it three or four times, memorably in Chicago, at The Mad Bar in 2000, where I was nearly laughed offstage, and in San Antonio later that year, where I came in second to Omelia Ortiz, one of the country's best slammers.

As for familiar venues, I'm lucky to live an hour's drive from Burlington, where until recently the Rhombus Gallery on College Street hosted slams the first and third Fridays of each month. Even with the Rhombus gone, slams continue to thrive in Burlington, and whenever I can, I make the hour's drive from my home to whatever café or bar is hosting a slam, rushing to sign up early and thus assure myself of one of the twelve slots. Typically I'll be carrying a new poem and a bag full of older poems, including those I've already performed too many times, at least in Vermont.

House rules in Burlington typically provide for twelve slammers in the first of two rounds. The top six scoring poets advance to round two, and these finalists start with fresh scores.

Round one offers a good opportunity to experiment with a new poem. Then for round two, I can unleash the incredible powers of a poem I know I can count on. If a new poem earns a high score, I'll consider it for the elevated status of a "round two poem" in later slams. I'll rehearse it enough to learn it by heart (I do not "memorize" it, a key distinction mentioned before), freeing my hands of a manuscript and of course providing enhanced opportunities for meaningful eye contact. Once I know the poem by heart, I can rehearse in the car on my way to a slam, watching the second hand of the dashboard clock. If I can say the poem assuredly and with clear enunciation in 2:15 or 2:30, it's fairly safe to assume I can perform it publicly in fewer than three minutes.

With longer poems I look for extraneous lines or stanzas to cut, a heart-wrenching exercise for me, but necessary. What a pleasure it is to perform these same poems in nonslam circumstances, without the three-minute constraint, to paste back in the beloved lines, the extra couple of unnecessary laughs! I'm also playing with ways to anticipate surprise, and this is crazy, but it's fun. If a siren or a bell tower clock's bonging drifted through the venue's open window at a crucial moment in my backwards poem, I'd say, "sirens sucked back to the source of their sound" or "the big bells' bonging brought back to their clappers," but the appropriate moments have yet to materialize. Obsessive planning for the unlikely coincidence is nuts, but I would always hope to have sufficient presence in my poem to respond in keeping to the moment without breaking stride. There's nothing worse than the agony of realizing, after the fact, "I should have ... "

I do have a moment, recorded by luck on videotape, when a cat hopped onto the riser at the old Pyralisk Gallery, in Montpelier, Vermont, as I was reading the lines "Your headlights catch the eyes of a cat working the roadside ..." and someone in the audience called out, "FIX!" In forty years of reading and performing my poems, this was the one time when a lovely coincidence enhanced the moment. An even more serendipitous experience would be to react to an unexpected event with a creative, spontaneous response that comes from within the voice of the poem, the act of writing at the moment of performance.

Discover Writing Press   www.discoverwriting.com   © 2005

Freestyling

When preparing for a slam becomes a drag, and you're tired of hauling home the first-place cash prizes with the poems anyone with a brain is tired of hearing you perform so flawlessly, try freestyling.

This takes guts. I've done it, and did it well once, the other times turning in fluent but unimportant language delivered in search of meaning. I will continue to try it at appropriate moments – usually when there's nothing to lose. In my one successful attempt – at the Nationals in Providence, 2000 – several sideshow venues featured various theme slams throughout the day, and I entered one for freestyling. When the slammaster called me to the stage and declared "provolone" and "blood pressure medicine" as my key words, I already had an opening line in mind that would allow me to stall as I found a way to incorporate the surprise words from the audience. "Whatever shall we do with Robert?" is how I would start my poem, posing a question that would then entertain whatever my surprise topics would be. I fudged a couple of lines about Robert, who was hungry for a good slice of bologna, engaging the audience by disappointing expectation that it would be provolone, and eventually settled on my ability to

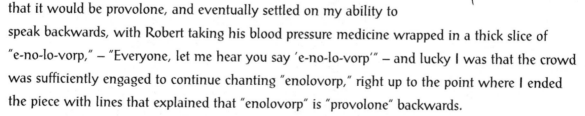

speak backwards, with Robert taking his blood pressure medicine wrapped in a thick slice of "e-no-lo-vorp," – "Everyone, let me hear you say 'e-no-lo-vorp'" – and lucky I was that the crowd was sufficiently engaged to continue chanting "enolovorp," right up to the point where I ended the piece with lines that explained that "enolovorp" is "provolone" backwards.

Next time I freestyle, I think I'll employ the opening question gambit, and see whether the disappointed expectation of approaching, but avoiding, the subject will allow an opportunity to

again introduce the backwards concept. The real trick will lie in keeping the language flowing and meaningful; using these preset gambits might allow for better focus on tying it all together.

I am in awe of the many freestylers who have developed the skill of providing hip-hop rhythms and corresponding rhyme to verses they compose on the spot. Talk about composing in a pressure cooker!

Trust a Reader, but Maybe Not an Audience

In my view, masterpieces of the page are hard to convey onstage. They are masterpieces either because they employ a driving rhythm that becomes too obvious when performed or, more likely, because they convey ideas and images that are best appreciated in the recursive act of reading and rereading. It's tedious to hear a poet attempting to re-create the shape of a poem by pausing at the end of each line; better to perform for meaning, not art.

For me, the choice is simple: When possible, work on a narrative poem, ideally with some understated humor, and with an iambic closing that fools the judges into thinking they've just heard poetry. Look for poems that play to an audience, not to the art of poetry, until the final couple of lines.

Microphones

Experience with microphones provides the best way to gauge whether use of a mike is the right choice in the varied venues of slam. Of course where no mike is available, there's no decision to be made. And, when there is no mike, it becomes especially important for the slammer not to move or speak (at which point the timekeeper's clock starts ticking) until the audience is completely still. Waiting for this moment can seem endless, but if the audience is restless, they are unlikely to be as aware as the person onstage of the passage of time. Let them come to you; to try to hush an audience not only starts the clock, it diminishes the dignity of the performer, and the performer simultaneously loses the effect of calm drama building that is almost always inherent in performances where the slammer knows this simple trick. It projects confidence, perhaps even mastery. Even when a microphone is available, this dramatic pause is preferable

to hushing the audience with the poem's opening lines or bullying people to silence because the mike affords such power.

And, when there is a microphone, one has the option of standing beside or in front of the mike, often an excellent strategy if others have been performing on mike. There's something more direct in the unamplified voice, more sincere. The disadvantage is one's loss of the range of volume, from a whisper to an easy shout, that a good sound system can convey to audiences of any size.

Certainly in almost any small coffeehouse or gallery, my choice, regardless of others' decisions, is to perform off mike. I view anything that comes between the audience and me as an impediment. I want to get out from behind podiums and microphones; I want to take enough steps forward, even when it means climbing down off the stage, to get as close as possible to my audience. Only considerations of eye contact keep me on a riser or stage in a large venue; only considerations of audibility impel me to step behind a microphone; only considerations of spreading out a manuscript or pile of books allow me to contemplate a podium and, in those rare cases, I'm scheming strategies for stepping out from behind those barriers.

Indeed, another disadvantage of a microphone is that it pretty much requires the slammer to stay in one place. Of course, this isn't always such a bad thing. On most occasions when I've seen slammers remove the mike from its stand, thus burdening one hand with the task of holding the mike, the movement has not been meaningful enough to warrant the appearance of a rock star strutting the stage.

For novice slammers, the microphone may serve as an anchor, keeping them from drifting or pacing without apparent purpose. Any movement beyond that of eyes and mouth is distracting – unless it has a purpose that relates to the poem. Scratching one's nose has purpose, but unless the poem makes reference to a tickly nose, it's best to endure the itch.

Whenever possible, scout the venue before a slam. Check out whether a mike is available and necessary, study sight lines, determine where in the room is the best place to sit, and where the ideal performance spot is. If possible, take your place onstage, whether it is an actual stage or simply your concept of the best place from which to perform. If it involves a microphone, it's important to learn to operate and adjust the mike smoothly, without undue complaint from the

PAGE
79

microphone itself or feedback from the sound engineer. What nut do you loosen to tilt or raise or lower the mike? How close to the mike can you be without popping your p's? How far from the mike can you stand without losing all amplification?

Finally, take it from me: Observe the mike cord. When I entered a slam in San Antonio as the mysterious stranger, using the microphone skillfully in a noisy, crowded bar, I kept my cool almost to the end of the second round, when I managed to intertwine my right foot with the power cord and, leaving the stage to thunderous applause and utter adulation, silenced the crowd by dragging the bottom of the mike stand out from under the microphone, which went down with the amplified crashing of a lassoed bull buffalo. Perhaps this affected the judges' scores negatively, for my total score fell well below a perfect thirty!

In summary, the more experience one can get with a microphone the better. Nothing irritates judges more than electronic squealing, clunking, or a voice that is screaming, amplified to the point of pain.

Chapter 8: The Nationals

I have been to two Nationals, in Providence as an alternate for Vermont's 2000 team and in Seattle in 2001 as a competing member of the team. Still a neophyte to the national slam scene, I admit that my impressions may exhibit naïveté or bias beyond what I have already displayed.

In two years at the Nationals, I was once moved to tears. In Providence, the high school slam, held in a church basement three blocks from slam central, offered two or three heart-wrenching performances that made me feel that every one of my thirty-five years of teaching had been super-ficial. One poem, performed by a girl with a strong Puerto Rican accent, detailed the struggles of a family, new to the United States, who loved their new country but suffered for being "differ-ent." Throughout the slam I celebrated the fact that here were students who had found a voice to express the truths of their lives – and without the bravado of the master slammers. I **believed** what I was hearing and seeing: if these were "performances," they were highly controlled. This contrasted with my general impression of the adult performances, where emotions often seemed contrived.

It's a minor honor for a city to win the position of host to a national slam, although I'm told no city goes through the same shenanigans to act as slam host as those observed when the Olympic sites are selected! Providence and Seattle both seemed aware of the somewhat eccentric assemblage that wandered their streets and alleys, looking for the plethora of venues: cafés and classrooms, basements and restaurants, bars, and church anterooms turned over to four or five days of featured bouts as well as the sideshow bouts, which is where I found the greatest delights.

Again in Providence, in 2000, at a prop slam in one of the side venues, I witnessed two performances that, while perhaps short on poetry, would nevertheless haunt anyone's memory. A poem of self-realization was accompanied by the shedding of a toga to reveal an entirely naked poet, tears flowing, exhorting her audience to look at her as who she was, and the other a poet with a puppet about half as large as himself and identical in every detail. This alter ego added a

PAGE
81

voice to the poem, and climaxed the performance by spraying the first and second rows of the astonished (and grossed out) audience. As I remember, that performance earned a perfect thirty in a late-night barroom slam that left a lot of us speechless as we staggered back up the crooked streets of Providence to the campus of Johnson and Wales, which was providing dormitory space to participants.

Okay, broad strokes from a biased neophyte. Average age is probably late twenties, people of all colors and ethnic backgrounds, urban, suburban, and rural people of all genders with a generous representation of people who are open and, somewhat tirelessly, public about their political outrage at attitudes toward their specific minority group. My guess is that fewer than one percent would call themselves Bush Republicans.

Within this environment, it is safe to declare one's "differences" from the stage; I'm glad this is the case, but I lament the number of poems whose sole point seems to be just that. Perhaps half of the poems I heard at the Nationals addressed ethnicity or sexuality to the exclusion of other topics. For the one-time slam-goer, this may be okay, but for weeklong audiences, for fellow slammers, it breeds monotony. Or am I the old "coach" again, out of step with my "peers"!

Poetry Slam, Inc., which organizes the Nationals, does an excellent job of selecting host cities, presumably based on the strength of the host's capacity to locate and staff ten or twelve venues for five days of continuous slam activity. In Providence, a free breakfast was available to every registered slammer; in Seattle, a spacious restaurant/bar offered us its full menu at half price (food only!), twenty-four hours a day. It also served as host to a round-the-clock poetry marathon, an attempt at a new record for the **Guinness Book of World Records.**

Major bouts are held in the evening at four or six sites, but the most fun, for me, were the unofficial daytime slams at the outlying venues: the haiku slam, the youth slam, the prop slam, the freestyle and cover slams, the queer slam, the "fifth-wheel" (alternates') slam. Except for the fifth-wheel slam, all these slams are open to all comers, whether members of a team or attending the Nationals as coaches, alternates, or groupies. These are the slams where people take the greatest risks and where, because the stakes are low, they perform most spontaneously.

The Nationals have a small group of acknowledged superstars, many of them immortalized

in the 1996 documentary film, **Slam Nation**. Highly gifted performers/poets, they perform on teams that usually make it to the semifinals or the finals, and they are sometimes as capable of astounding physical feats as they are, without question, capable of thoughtful, moving poetry. For a stranger to slam, I'd recommend finals night as the quintessential slam experience, encouraging that same stranger to arrive six hours early, thus having time to sample, and perhaps enter, one or two of the unofficial slams and, with special luck, to find the teen slam for an inspiring view of the future of poetry.

Discover Writing Press   www.discoverwriting.com   © 2005

APPENDIX
The Best Slam Resources

Web sites:

www.poetryslam.com The official Web site of Poetry Slam Incorporated, host of the National Poetry Slam. Excellent resource for anyone interested in slam, with a fairly comprehensive bookstore and a useful directory of more than one hundred slam venues across the country.

www.e-poets.net "An Incomplete History of Slam" is a useful extended essay on slam's history and its prospects. Here's an excerpt: "Slam's evangelism is very much like that of the Beats'. Both poetry movements took their own promotion seriously, and insinuated promotion into many things they did. A difference, however, is that Slam poets ride the 'Information Superhighway' and use jet travel instead of jumping in a car to go 'On the Road.' The rise of connectedness among slam poets, and slam poetry's rapid ability to jump across national frontiers intact, was never before enjoyed and practiced so widely by any preceding movement of writers. E-mail and the web are thus a kind of cultural glue for the slam movement, binding so many dispersed people into shared experiences." (Copyright 2000, Kurt Heintz)

www.upwordspoetry.com   Connecticut slammer and master organizer of youth slams Elizabeth Thomas has created this terrific resource for slammers, teachers, and, especially, young poets. Included are a list of useful poem starters, regularly updated information on the annual national youth poetry slam, Brave New Voices, a comprehensive list of publishing/ performance opportunities for young writers and some of the same for older poets.

www.thewordsmithpress.com   An excellent source of books and CDs by the nation's best slam poets, this Web site provides a listing of major forthcoming events, a reading room filled with advice on all matters involving performance, publication, and slam, and links to other helpful Web sites.

www.itvs.org/poeticlicense/index.html A Web site dedicated to providing young writers with a complete set of resources. Includes writing exercises, a chat room for teachers, curriculum suggestions, and lists of youth literary groups.

www.slampapi.com The Web site of slam's inventor, Marc Kelly Smith. Especially fascinating is the editorial "Slam Hypocrisy," by high school junior Adam Martin, in which the author launches a heartfelt complaint against hypocrisy among slammers and judges at a national youth slam in Ann Arbor.

www.slamnation.com Video segments, reviews, and links to the featured performers on the definitive slam documentary film.

Videos:

Slam Nation The definitive slam video, this features performances at the 1996 National Poetry slam in Portland, Oregon. $29.95 from Poetry Slam Incorporated: info@poetryslam.com

The 2000 National Poetry Slam Finals Another colorful video, this one presents amazing performances from the 2000 Finals at Providence, Rhode Island. $24.95 from Poetry Slam Incorporated: info@poetryslam.com

Slammin' The television pilot produced by Paul Devlin, who made **Slam Nation.** This video follows five slammers in a single competition. $24.95 from Poetry Slam Incorporated: info@poetryslam.com

Books:

Top Secret Slam Strategies, by Taylor Mali. Words Worth Ink. A lighthearted and comprehensive guide to winning slams, with a special focus on the Nationals. Anecdotes and practical advice. $8 from Poetry Slam Incorporated: info@poetryslam.com

Poetry Slam: The Competitive Art of Performance Poetry, edited by Gary Glazner. Manic D Press. Documents ten years of the slam movement, including 100 slam winning poems, with tips on slam strategy and setting up a national tour. $14.95 from Poetry Slam Incorporated: info@poetryslam.com

Freedom to Speak, edited by Scott Woods. The Wordsmith Press. An anthology of fifty poems from the 2002 National Poetry Slam with a CD containing twenty-three of the best performances from that same event. $15 from Poetry Slam Incorporated: info@poetryslam.com

Outsiders, edited by Laure-Anne Bosselaar. Milkweed Editions. Many poems in this anthology will engage young readers, offering several choices for a cover slam.

The Voice That Is Great Within Us, edited by Hayden Carruth. Bantam Books. Last century's definitive collection of modern and contemporary (to 1970) poetry.

DISCOVER WRITING PRESS

To view our other titles and
to order additional copies of

HEWITT'S GUIDE
to SLAMPoetry
&
PoetrySLAM

visit our website at

www.discoverwriting.com

phone: 1-800-613-8055
fax: 1-802-897-2084

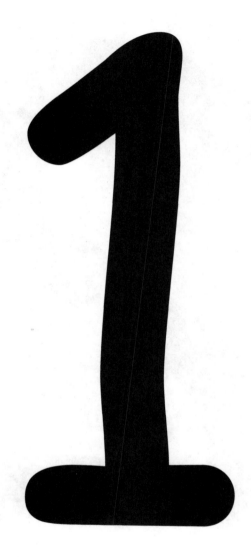